Christmas, 1981

To: John Elmon
With best wishes.

Tracy Herrick

Timing

HOW TO
PROFITABLY
MANAGE MONEY AT
DIFFERENT STAGES
OF YOUR
LIFE.

TIMING

TRACY G. HERRICK

ARGUS COMMUNICATIONS
One DLM Park
Allen, Texas 75002

ACKNOWLEDGMENTS

I am grateful for the excellent suggestions and encouragement from experts in the field of psychology and personal money management. I particularly appreciate the advice of the following friends who should share the good points of this book.

Mr. C. Derek Anderson, President, C. D. Anderson & Co., Inc.
Securities trading

Mr. T. Clayton Bowen, CPA
Accountant

Mr. William Dobbs, C.L.U., The Equitable Life Assurance Society of the United States
Insurance counsellor

Mr. Edwin Hatherly, M.A., partner, Bodin, Emling and Hatherly
Psychologist, Career counsellor

Mr. James G. Maletis, Morgan Stanley & Co., Inc.
Securities advisor

Mr. John Murden, President, Louis Allen & Co., Inc.
Management consultant

Mr. Reed Bingham, Senior Vice President, Jefferies & Co., Inc.
Securities trading

Mrs. Marlene Prendergast, LLB
Attorney

Mr. David Rahn, Executive Vice President, Bailard, Biehl & Kaiser, Inc.
Investment advisor

(Continued on page 255)

FIRST EDITION

Printed in the United States of America.

Argus Communications
A Division of DLM, Inc.
One DLM Park
Allen, Texas 75002

International Standard Book Number: 0-89505-062-5
Library of Congress Number: 81-69111

Contents

Introduction

WHY YOU NEED TO MANAGE YOUR MONEY

Money has an important purpose in your life. It is the means by which you can achieve your fullest human potential.

Most often, however, money is erroneously considered as a goal. You often hear people say that they want to make more money or save more money or spend more money. These goals mistate the relationship between a person and money, and those goals can lead to warped or even barren personal lives, replete with missed opportunities.

Money should develop you. It should be the means by which you can search into your own nature and promote your talents to their fullest.

Many people go to extremes in their use of money. Some accumulate money out of fear that they might be without it. Others disregard it by spending it with abandon. A few renounce it, leading almost monastic lives in the belief that money is something awful. But none of these ways of using money leads to a fulfilling life.

The key to personal money management links money to the development of your fullest potential—which is what this book is about. Your money management should enable you to realize your personal goals. These goals include those which you hold closely, as well as those that you have worked out from discussion with your family and friends. Some of your goals may include ones that you have not fully recognized, and may lie beyond your present vision. You may have not had enough experience to come to grips with them or you may deliberately not wish to face them. Yet to neglect these kinds of personal goals is to keep part of you in the shadow.

Money management should, first and last, help you become what you want to be. It should help you find out who you really are. It should enable you to unleash the powers inside you by laying back the obstacles created by your lack of experience, your fears, or perhaps the circumstances of your early years. Any other use of money is a waste.

Of course, this is easier to say than to do. Money has rules and conventions. It is like everything else shared among people. You need to understand these rules, just as a person needs to understand language to communicate. But since the use, not the study, of language creates literature, so your understanding of money management is only a beginning. You need to use money correctly as you strive to realize its benefits.

This book looks at money from a personal point of view and does not try to solve the question of the future direction of financial markets. Nevertheless, as you progress through selected stages of your life cycle, you will be able to understand certain of the financial markets better and decide whether they are valued cheaply or expensively. You will learn that there is a time for every type of investment, particularly as it relates to your life.

How you should manage your money depends on your personal goals and your response to your stage in the life cycle. You will then need to adapt the rules of money to your personal needs.

Your job in managing money is to not let anything knock out your desire to develop yourself. That's the goal. Personal financial management simply provides the resources to accomplish what you need to become yourself.

PART *I*
OVERVIEW OF THE LIFE CYCLE AND MONEY MANAGEMENT

Chapter 1

THE FINANCIAL
CHALLENGES OF YOUR
LIFE CYCLE

*T*HERE is nothing new about the idea of personal life cycle. It has long been a theme in literature and art. Shakespeare pointed out 400 years ago that there were stages to a person's life. The idea of a life cycle has been a common theme in other literature and painting. Cervantes, the author of *Don Quixote,* was deeply involved with the subject in his writings, and Michelangelo's sculpture is a portrayal of certain of these stages.

Today, the concept of a personal life cycle has been rediscovered by clinical psychologists, including Carl Jung, Daniel Levinson, and Erik Erikson. The idea of a life cycle for each person is one whose time has come again.

THE STAGES OF THE LIFE CYCLE

I have observed that there are three complete cycles in each person's lifetime. The cycles involve basic, recurring themes. Nevertheless, during each cycle there are new and different aspects of personal development that are emphasized. The life cycle may be considered to be a description of how we create a new understanding of ourselves, as well as purge ourselves of our faulty past perceptions of our nature. Through this process of personal development, the most durable part of our nature comes to the foreground.

The first cycle covers the period from childhood to adolescence. This is a period of development of our personal identity. The second cycle includes the period from our adulthood to midlife. It is the period when we explore and develop our human and economic skills. The third cycle includes our maturity and old age. It is the period when we explore and develop the skills that perpetuate our culture. These three cycles give us an opportunity to look at ourselves in new and different perspectives. It is as if we have three times in our lives to explore and develop who we are.

There are two stages to each of the three complete cycles. The first stage is a period of exploration, when a person learns new understandings of people and working skills. The second stage is a period of integration, when a person comes to grips with determining which skills and understanding fit his or her character. During the first stage of each cycle, we learn, without much personal discrimination, about the world we live in. During the subsequent stage, we intensify our awareness of knowledge that has personal meaning, and we discard the rest, sometimes rebelliously.

The age that pertains to a particular stage varies for each person, and the ages indicated here are meant only to be approximate. During the first of the six stages, the period of childhood, money management is of only minor importance, since virtually all financial decisions are made by adults.

Thus there are five adult stages that cover the period when a person makes decisions concerning money.

Adolescence: 14 to 22 Years of Age

This is the period when a person discovers a new personal world. The person differentiates from his or her original family and sees himself or herself as an individual for the first time.

The financial issues of this stage involve a strategy to spend money to learn skills. Education is critically important, but education should be construed in a broader sense than formal studies and should include apprenticeship and other work-related learning experiences. Borrowing for a learning experience is usually money well spent if savings or gifts from the family are not available. This is a time for establishing a credit record and a long-term relationship with a bank.

Adulthood: 23 to 35 Years of Age

During this stage a person finds a mate and consolidates a career. It is a period of nurturing a family and sensing how to adapt oneself to the business of making a living. There is an emphasis on perfecting skills, rather than searching for new directions.

This stage emphasizes a financial strategy of building up assets. It is a period to use leverage to expand a financial base. Long-term payback periods are not usually a problem, if the investments are well conceived.

Time is on one's side during this period, since long-term positions will often reap major benefits. Yet these positions need to be tempered with the need to build a savings base and not build up a high breakeven point in a budget that leaves little cushion for unexpected difficulties.

Midlife: 36 to 50 Years of Age

During this stage, a person discovers the unique inner world of the mind. It is a period of personal discoveries, as well as the re-emergence of ideas that have long remained dormant. It is also a period of rebellious integration, when whatever is not accepted is purged.

The financial strategy is to build liquidity and to keep personal expenses as low as possible. Spending should support a search for new understandings and the quest for new directions. A person should be prepared to liquidate assets to further this exploration. Liquidity provides a financial base of greatest flexibility and is compatible with a budget that has a low breakeven point. Tax planning is important, because it holds one of the keys to understanding whether the work and skills of the previous adult period are being channeled in the right direction.

Maturity: 51 to 65 Years of Age

Interests focus on nurturing one's friends and family during this period of the life cycle. There is a special emphasis on people rather than things. There is a strong interest in passing the torch of knowledge and experience to others. This is the period of mentors and great teachers. There is a ruthlessness with the use of time, and unimportant activities are pruned.

During this period, the financial emphasis is to build up assets, and to take a long-term view of the future. The long-term view is, however, not as long as that of the adulthood stage. There is less time remaining for reaping the benefits of leverage. Thus real estate investments diminish in importance relative to other types of investments. The experience of previous years gives a person perspective for choosing equities of strong companies, and for looking at venture capital situations which might develop successfully within a decade.

In this manner, experience and knowledge may be used as a type of leverage.

Age and Simplicity: 66 Years of Age and Onward

This is a period when intuitive capabilities develop along with a recognition of the importance of simplicity to all aspects of life. It is also the stage when the spirit asserts itself over one's physical deterioration and struggle returns. It is a time for consolidating what is most important about a life and a culture, and a time for seeing how the important treasures of experience and accomplishment can be perpetuated.

During this stage, money should be spent as it is received. There is no need for new long-term investments, nor is there a need for special efforts to save. Liquidity is important, since changes in one's personal situation can occur suddenly. Living expenses should be kept low, but in response to the challenge of the period, spending for learning and education should increase.

IMPORTANCE OF THE LIFE CYCLE

Your life cycle is perhaps the most important thread of your life. It ties together the wide variety of opportunities that you will likely experience and explore. It is a master guide that gives you the scope of the personal environment you will travel through.

The process of living is discovering who we are. The life cycle points out that each stage has certain challenges, and these challenges enable us to understand ourselves. Although the broad outlines of the life cycle appear to be similar for most people, the way in which each person responds is always unique. Success in our personal development is mastering these challenges of our life cycle as they occur.

Many talents today are wasted because of a lack of financial support. We often speak of our great abundance, and the wealth of our country. But for many people, this is not correct. A large number of people have only an insignificant surplus after their expenses are paid. In a financial sense, they are no different from poor people who inhabit most of the globe. The wealth that surrounds us in the last quarter of the twentieth century does not enable as many to develop talents as it should. The problem is not that wealth is lacking, but that many people don't recognize the need for money management to provide the basis for that development, which always is a personal issue.

The life cycle suggests that there will be three times in your life when you can search for an understanding of your uniqueness, and in your own way, your genius. These stages are adolescence, midlife, and the age and simplicity. These are stages when you can make discoveries about yourself that will ultimately give you great personal strength and great happiness. Yet this search requires a financial surplus. It is difficult to concentrate on your personal development if bill collectors are sending you threatening letters or calling you at dinner time. You need to provide for the financial basis of your development, or it may not occur.

The periods of restoration are the stages of adulthood and maturity. During these stages you use your knowledge and skills to enrich the people around you. You also refill your financial reservoir.

Money can be used for many purposes. It can be used for power, for show, as well as for personal development. Once the purpose of providing payment for the basic needs of life has been fulfilled, the latter use of money becomes important. It requires self-control to look at money as a vehicle for your personal development. But nothing is more important as a personal objective, once your basic needs of sustaining life are fulfilled.

Chapter 2

YOUR THREE MONEY PRINCIPLES

*M*OST conscientious money managers have developed money management principles to manage money effectively on a long-term basis. You need money management principles, too, if you expect to use money in an effective manner.

Three principles are fundamental to money management. Any person can succeed in money management by following them. They are: (1) make flexible financial decisions, (2) build a surplus to finance the needs of successive periods of your life cycle, and (3) keep money decisions personal. These principles remain unchanged throughout the life cycle stages. They are the central pivots around which the financial aspects of the life cycle revolve.

These principles are really demanding taskmasters. They serve as a screen to separate out the most durable ideas.

Nevertheless, whenever a discussion of money management comes to the issue of principles, someone almost always says, "What you say may make sense now, but suppose we have a major inflation or a depression or even a war?" It doesn't matter whether there are good times or bad times.

These principles will work for you, and if you follow them, they won't fail you.

Make Financial Decisions That Are Flexible

Financial decisions need to be flexible, because needs change over time. A decision that was right for you at age thirty may not be best for you at age forty. Financial decisions need to be flexible so that a decision made at an earlier age does not impinge on your development at a later stage in the life cycle.

It is almost always possible to change or amend a financial decision. The nature of financial markets permits this flexibility, since almost everything can be bought or sold. The key is to be able to change a financial decision without a loss. This means that in making major investments you will be guided not only by your personal preferences but also by preferences of the market. You will have one eye on your tastes and interests and another on the tastes and interests of a large proportion of potential buyers. In this manner your assets will be marketable.

A number of people find this principle somewhat offensive. Some may think of themselves as being superior or different from mass-market tastes and may wish to surround themselves with personal and financial assets which they believe are more fitting to their personal standards. Other persons may wish to avoid any association with the mainstream of American culture, and they may seek assets that serve as a symbol of separateness, or even of defiance. Still other persons consider themselves taste-setters and they desire the newest articles to give themselves an identification with trends.

It is possible to retain your individuality, even to surround yourself with an unusual culture, and still retain good business judgment. One solution is to rent or lease the major assets that you show to your friends and to the world but buy assets that are marketable. Yet this solution does not often work for people who handle their assets personally.

For example, few people have bought an apartment that is highly marketable and conventional in design, yet have lived in a rented or leased home or apartment designed with exotic or unconventional taste, and have handled all the the transactions personally. Nevertheless, there is no reason why this approach couldn't be useful if a business manager handled the finances. In fact, trust departments of banks are accustomed to working with similar situations, in which children or grandchildren have adopted unconventional life styles, all of which are supported by the most orthodox types of investments. Of course, this approach requires assets that are large enough to pay for the services of a money manager, and still leave funds intact for investment.

A second approach is to invest in the classics of finance. The classics are not difficult to identify. In architecture, Georgian design is usually considered classic. In stocks, any of the the nation's largest corporations which provide basic products or services essential for national defense would qualify. Among precious metals and minerals, gold is the best example. Everybody recognizes these investments, and there will be a market for these investments under all economic conditions. Even within these classic investments there is a considerable range for personal preferences For example, an investment in Hewlett-Packard common stock represents a much different type of investment than an investment in gold coins. Yet both are examples of a classic approach to investments.

The third approach toward ensuring the marketability of an investment is to select only the best and unique types of investment. This approach requires talent and knowledge of these markets by the investor. It also requires a thorough knowledge of the conditions of the market for these investments. For example, I know of one investor who has specialized in rebuilding and collecting Franklin automobiles. (The Franklin is an unusual, air-cooled antique automobile. The manufacturer went out of business in the depression of the 1930s.) This person has become well-known among the many hundreds of collectors of these automobiles. These cars have increased in value rapidly, and this person has benefited from an ability to discern rebuildable cars. His investments in these old cars are based on price trends in the antique car market. He tells me he could sell his complete inventory of cars in a day, and he has at least two bids for each car. He understands value, customers, and tastes in his specialty market.

Making financial decisions that are flexible means avoiding personal indulgences or taking extreme positions. For example, it would be a mistake to buy a house that would be difficult to resell in the belief that you would intend to live in it for a lifetime. It would also be a mistake to live by a personal budget at age 25 that was designed to prepare you for retirement at age 65.

The two key determinates of marketability are time and price. These factors work against each other. For example, as you increase your asking price for an asset, the time needed to sell it lengthens. Conversely, as you lower your asking price, the asset will be sold more quickly. There are certain exceptions, such as highly specialized designer products, but the rule holds in most instances. Making investments more marketable usually has the effect of increasing the number of potential buyers, which increases the likelihood that a sale will be made.

The stages of life require the successive creation of new financial goals. Along with those changes in financial goals, assets need to be built up, subsequently liquidated in part or totally, and later again built up. Each period of building assets is different, and each stage of the life cycle builds on different types of assets.

Most people see this development vividly on a personal basis. Ideals and personal mentors change. Money management requires a similar adaptability to change. But many people do not recognize that their spending patterns will change as dramatically as their personal life. There is a time to save and a time to spend.

Most people sense the need for flexibility with their work and their home. But they seldom consider the need to be so flexible with their money management. Moreover, most people do not regard their money as being interrelated with their personal development. Yet the two are interrelated. Both must be flexible. The life cycle is a description of growing up and developing as a person. It is the personal story of how each person responds to the stereotypes of the first dozen years, tests them, and step by step replaces them with personal knowledge. Managing your money should provide you with the means to do this. If you do not make your money serve these personal needs, the failure is not only financial, it is also personal, and that is the greater tragedy.

Build a Surplus to Finance the Needs of Successive Life-Cycle Periods

The development of financial surplus does not mean that you need to accumulate great wealth. It does mean that you need enough income to take care of the basic necessities of food, clothing, and shelter, with enough income remaining to support your personal development. This surplus is the most important money in your possession.

One friend grew up as a young man during the depression of the 1930s. I first met him when he was an adult in his forties. He often spoke of his interest in engineering. He had graduated from high school, and had attended two night-school courses at a local engineering school. But he never continued his studies in a dedicated manner. He often remarked that he had been deeply shaken by the depression of the 1930s and had taken a job with a local utility because it was secure. The job was clerical, and he never regarded it as being challenging or important. He married a girl whose parents were well-to-do and who gave his family money whenever they were unable to make ends meet. These parents gave him the down payment for their house, their car, and as each of three children arrived, looked after them financially.

Once when he was talking about his high regard for engineers, I asked him why he had not pursued his own education more earnestly. He said that he could not afford the expense. I never believed that answer. He had permitted himself to live beyond his means and had accepted regular gifts from his wife's parents. If he had lived in a less expensive home, had used public transportation, cut back his expenditures and worked out a budget with his wife where she would have spent less, I am sure that he could have provided for his family and put enough money aside to pay for night-school tuition. Moreover, his attitude toward his job would have improved, and he would have looked at his job as an important stepping stone to a future career either within the utility or with an engineering company. But he never felt the pride of accomplishment from getting control over his budget. The subsidies from his wife's parents were too convenient and permitted him to believe that he was enjoying the present, while his hopes for an engineering future were little more than an old dream. The surplus wasn't there, but it could have been achieved.

All of this took place years before the welfare programs of today. Yet this really is a welfare story. This person did not believe that he could reduce his standard of living and still retain his sense of dignity. In fact, he could have done so. And if he had taken that step and used the surplus to obtain an engineering education, he would have earned far more money than his clerical duties gave him.

Our present welfare program is doing the same thing to an important segment of our population. For people who are old, incapacitated, or handicapped, the welfare programs are humane and worthwhile. Yet for all other persons, these programs are really inhumane, since they tend to dull a person's recognition of the need to develop a financial surplus. The welfare program can dull a person's sense of control over money and his or her life cycle. These people are fine individuals as one meets them in casual conversation. But their personal accomplishments are only a fraction of what they might be.

Your financial surplus should be used to develop your talents. Sometimes the surplus and the development of skills occur simultaneously. A person who works while attending night school is an example of this. Sometimes the surplus reflects a gift, such as when a person's college bills are paid by a parent. More frequently, the surplus is built in one period and the use of the money to develop personal skills occurs at a later period. The link between the buildup of your capital during one period and the spending of this capital at another period is one of the most important financial challenges of the life cycle.

As has been mentioned, the life cycle alternates between periods of challenge and restoration. During each period there is a feeling that the current period will continue uninterrupted. Most people do not tell themselves that their strivings will lessen in a few years or, in another instance, that their routine will be broken. But that is exactly what will happen. You are being asked to take a further step and build a capital base that will amount to thousands of dollars. This capital base, moreover, is for a purpose you cannot specifically designate. You do not now know how it will be used. Yet this surplus will be important to you, because at certain periods of your life you will see yourself in a new light, and you will search for a way to develop your talents in ways you had never expected. You should not hold back this new spirit because of a lack of surplus to provide for its proper development.

A friend had spent 20 years in the securities business and had developed skills as a capable analyst, understood trading and execution of orders, and was a convincing salesman. He had all the ingredients of a successful broker. However, he had spent all the money he had made. He believed that this spending was necessary to attract customers. A few years ago, he had an unexpected opportunity to buy a major interest in a brokerage house that had encountered problems he was well qualified to correct. The stock market was at a low. He owned no property, and his financial assets were relatively small after margin payment. He was unable to raise the capital that would be needed to buy out the old owners, and the old owners did not want a number of limited partners who would add capital but remain silent in the management of the firm. If this friend had built a surplus of only 5 percent of his income during each of the twenty years of his career and had simply put the surplus in a bank account with an average of 4 percent annual interest (the average for the historical period), he would have been able to arrange the purchase. It was a sad moment when this friend realized, in his period of midlife challenge, that he would not be able to be an owner of this business and would probably spend the rest of his life working for a firm owned by persons who had built their surplus into capital.

One of the most successful wine companies in northern California was started by an immigrant from Tuscany, Italy, who was more disadvantaged than most of the people who are now considered at the poverty level. Speaking little English and having no surplus to start with, this person made his living working in the fields of a valley 70 miles north of San Francisco. His meager income as a farm hand barely provided for his family.

To build capital, he hauled cobblestones from nearby quarries to San Francisco, where he sold them for street paving. With the money he saved he went into winemaking. Starting small, he first bought one old redwood vat and a hand press for crushing grapes. On the basis of his ability to be successful in a small way, he attracted the interest of a local banker, who loaned him money to expand. The key that launched his successful winery was the accumulated surplus of several years' hauling of paving stones.

Many people mistakenly believe that they can borrow whatever amount of money they might need, thus believing that they do not need a surplus. In our time there has been a blurring between debt and capital, and many financial institutions have encouraged this confusion. But there is a fundamental difference. Debt always involves a promise for interest and usually repayment. A surplus involves no obligation for payment of any kind. A surplus is powerful money. It can be used adventurously, since it does not require a lender's approval. Most importantly, it can be used as a base on which debt can be built.

The importance of building a surplus has gone out of fashion with many people over the past three decades. The rate of savings in the United States has fallen to 4 percent recently, meaning the average person spends 96 percent of income and puts away 4 percent in some form of financial savings. That savings rate is almost half of the savings rate of three decades ago, and one-third to one-quarter that of more rapidly growing economies such as Germany or Japan. Savings, or the building of surplus, is no longer considered necessary, since social security, pensions, health programs, welfare, unemployment compensation, Medicare, and many other programs represent a type of insurance against adversity. Moreover, the policies of the government, through budget deficits and monetary stimulus, have eroded the value of many types of investments, as well as savings deposits of banks and other financial institutions. Many people believe that their government is encouraging them to spend, and they faithfully respond.

All of these points may be true, yet they miss the critical importance of a surplus in your life cycle. A surplus provides the key ingredient to the control of your budget. A surplus also gives you flexibility in your progression through your life cycle. Even if every other reason for building a surplus were invalid or irrelevant, those two reasons would be compelling enough.

Keep Money Decisions Personal

Money is usually considered highly impersonal. It bears no special identity to its owner. Cash, the most transferable form of money, bears no owner's identity at all. Although virtually all securities, assets, debts, and money instruments are identified by their owner, that identification is a procedural step only.

In fact, money is highly personal. Money is your most important resource for development, and you should keep your financial development aligned with your personal development. Money provides you with a resource to develop your personal talents. If it is used for any other purposes, it is being wasted.

Money, or income, is sometimes considered a reflection of a person's power within any organization. Higher income reflects higher office in these organizations, and higher office almost always involves greater political power. This political power is similar in all organizations. It is the ability to direct some part of the affairs of a large number of people. Many people have considered this power as a source of personal development, and some corporations actively promote that idea.

There is a fundamental problem with the use of power, rather than money, as a vehicle of personal development. Power is not often transferable outside a limited number of people, and your options are always more limited with power than money. Power is a more volatile type of currency than money. Political groups come and go, but money remains. Most importantly, power can never give you independence. You are always part of a political fabric, and at certain times independence is essential for personal development.

Many decisions that involve personal development typically have a generous and liberal effect. A person who is fulfilling his or her personal gifts is usually a more attractive person to be associated with, either as a spouse, friend, parent, or business associate. Keeping money decisions personal acts as a reminder that money is not the objective of a person's life. It is your use of money that gives meaning to money, and if you use money in this personal manner, you and those around you will benefit.

PART II
ESSENTIAL CONTROLS

Chapter 3

HOW TO PREPARE YOUR PERSONAL MONEY PROFILE

A money profile measures your financial position. This profile is essential if you are to see where you currently stand and to determine whether you have made progress. Without measurement, you would have no certain basis of knowing your financial bearings or of knowing your strengths and weaknesses.

Some people use hunches to give them financial bearings. They have a rough or a general idea of both their income after expenses and their assets and liabilities. Many of these people manage their money very well. Nevertheless, in virtually every instance of this type, the person almost always had earlier financial experience and was able to draw upon this knowledge to provide mental guideposts. But there are relatively few persons with this skill. Most people need to prepare their income statements and balance sheet regularly.

I am always surprised whenever I find someone who prepares a financial profile on a regular basis. The process is not what most people initially would regard as an enjoyable exercise. The first preparation of a financial profile is always slow and awkward. Most people do not like to organize their activities into a financial format. It seems too removed from the way that they live. However, once this psychological obstacle is overcome, the effort becomes easier.

Personal Money Profile
Budget for _____

Month _____

Income
Taxed According to Employee or
Passive Owner Status
  Wages or Salary of Husband
  Wages or Salary of Wife
  Interest Income
  Dividends
  Pension Income
  Other Income

                    Total $_____

Taxed According to Entrepreneur Status
  Income from Proprietorship Status
  Income from Corporation in Capacity
    as a Director
  Capital Gains or Losses from Sales
    of Assets

                    Total $_____

Tax Deferred or Not Taxed
  Income from Gifts
  Income from Shelters
  Income from Tax-Exempt Securities
  Income from Other

                    Total $_____
                    Total Income $_____

HOW TO PREPARE YOUR PERSONAL MONEY PROFILE

Expenses
Personal Consumption
  Rent
  Housing Operations, Interest on
    Mortgage
  Food
  Clothing
  Public Transportation and Auto
    Operation
  Medical
  Insurance
  Personal
  Entertainment
                              Total $_____

Personal Development
  Formal Education
  Skills Development
  Reconnaissance
  Books, Literature and Seminars
                              Total $_____

Savings Additions and Investments
  Checking Account
  Savings Account
  Home Ownership, Equity Additions
  Automobile Ownership,
    Equity Additions
  Stocks
  Bonds
  Other Real Estate
  Other Investments
                              Total $_____

Public Consumption
  Federal Income Tax
  Social Security Contributions
  State Income Tax
  Local Income Tax
  Sales and Expense Tax
  Real Estate and Other Taxes
                              Total $_____
                              Total Expenses   **$**_____

                              Net Income   **$**_____

Expenditures of Household
Family of Four—Wage Earner Age 35

Estimate Based on U.S. Department of Labor
and Federal Reserve Statistics
for 1977

Personal Consumption
Rent or Interest Expense on

Home Purchase		23.4%
Food		14.1
Clothing		4.4
Public Transportation or Auto Operations, Interest Expense		8.0
Medical		3.8
Insurance—Life		1.4
Personal		2.3
Entertainment		3.1
	Total	60.5%

Personal Development

Formal Education		1.0%
Skills Development		—
Reconnaissance		—
Books and Literature		.2
	Total	1.2%

Savings, Total Purchases of Investments

Checking Account		.4%
Savings Account		2.7
Home Ownership		7.0
Automobile Ownership		6.4
Stocks		1.5
Bonds		.8
Other Real Estate		—
Trusts		—
Other Investments		—
	Total	18.8%

Public Consumption

Federal Income Tax		11.5%
Social Security Contributions		4.6
State Income Tax		3.0
Other Taxes		.4
	Total	19.5%

Total Personal Income	100.0%

Personal Money Profile

Balance Sheet for _____

All Items Shown at Current Market Value

December 31, 19___

	DEC 31 PREVIOUS YEAR	DEC 31 CURRENT YEAR	CHANGE
Assets			
Cash			
Checking Account			
Savings Account			
Money Market Investments			
Treasury Bills			
Certificates of Deposit and Other Investments			
Marketable Notes and Bonds			
Stocks and Listed Securities			
Cash Surrender Value of Life Insurance			
Automobile, Other Vehicles			
Gold, Precious Metals			
Total Liquid Assets	$_____		
Mortgages Owned			
Money Due from Relatives and Friends			
Letter Stock and Ownership in Small Business			
Infrequently Traded Stock			
Home			
Apartment Building			
Commercial Property			
Land			
Paintings, Objects of Art			
Diamonds, Precious Minerals			
Collector Stamps			
Antiques			
Planes, Boats, Other Assets			
Present Value of Vested Retirement Benefits			
Other Illiquid Assets			
Total Illiquid Assets	$_____		
Total Assets	$_____		

Liabilities

Notes Payable Within 30 Days

Accounts and Bills Payable
Within 30 Days

Mortgage Payment Due
Within 30 Days

Debts to Relatives and
Friends Due Within 30 Days

Total Current Liabilities $_____

Notes Payable Due Over 30 Days

Accounts and Bills Payable
Due Over 30 Days

Debts to Relatives and
Friends Due Over 30 Days

Margin Account

Other Long-Term Debts

Income Tax Liability in
Excess of Withholding

Total Long-Term Liabilities $_____

Total Liabilities $_____

Net Worth

Total Assets Less Total Liabilities $_____

Why You Need a Money Profile

If you want to manage your money, you need to become intimately familiar with the key measures of financial performance. You should learn both your numbers and their financial format, so that you can easily recall them and think about them when you may not have your papers nearby. You want to be able to make plans and adjustments easily in your mind, and you will be able to do this only after you have mastered this financial language.

Your money profile is not a substitute for your hunches and ideas. Rather, your money profile provides you with the best way of taking the next step and measuring that step. By measuring and comparing your plans, you can better evaluate which plan is best. Your overall evaluation will then give you a more complete and better understanding of your total money situation.

Many people make major financial commitments without looking at them in light of their money profile. One friend is a refugee from a Communist country. He had worked long hours, and despite a low-paying job, had accumulated several thousand dollars. This person hoped to buy a house, using his savings as a down payment, and sought my help in obtaining a mortgage. His savings would have provided a partial down payment, and he would have needed a second mortgage. The friend was very much interested in pursuing the purchase of the home. He had lived for several years in a home subsidized in part by a church group, and he felt that he should relinquish the home for others. Moreover, he had seen property values rise at a rapid rate, and he wanted to own a home which he hoped would also rise rapidly in value. However, the purchase of the house would have required monthly payments that would have been four times his rental payments, and those payments would have consumed virtually all his family income. He simply could not purchase the house using financing that was not government subsidized, and the latter type of financing was not available. It was only after he looked at his money profile that this simple fact became clear.

Although that door was closed, this person's money profile showed another door which could open. His balance sheet was free of debt, and his savings could be leveraged to buy a small business. It seemed clear that advancement would be slow in his present job with a custodial company. Perhaps he would be able to buy or start up a custodial company, using his savings, and thereby increase his income to a level where he could afford the monthly payments of a house purchase. These new avenues became apparent only after his money profile was reviewed. It showed his financial strengths and his limitations, and it pinpointed which directions he should take. It was a very practical and, at the same time, a very imaginative exercise.

The money profile outlined here is different from budgets which are available in most books and magazines on the subject of personal money management. The money profile shown here provides you with a basis of financial control, which is discussed in the next chapter. This profile also emphasizes spending patterns that are important to your personal development but that are relatively small in size. Because of their small proportion, they are often overlooked or not given the attention they deserve. For example, the amount of money you spend for education in a lifetime is only a small fraction of the amount you spend for housing. Nevertheless, the amount of money you spend for education has an enormous effect on your future, whereas small changes in the amount of your housing expenditures have virtually no effect on your future.

HOW TO PREPARE YOUR INCOME STATEMENT

The accompanying table shows 39 items of a typical budget of income and expenses that have been divided into seven main sections. These sections are: (1) income taxed according to employee status, (2) income taxed according to entrepreneur status, (3) income tax deferred or not taxed, (4) personal consumption, (5) personal development, (6) savings or purchase of investments, and (7) public consumption.

Your first step in preparing your income statement is to list your income and spending in the format of the accompanying table as accurately as possible. Most people do not have complete records of their monthly spending totals for each category. They need to assemble this information as the month progresses.

It is important to begin with an accurate position of where you stand in your spending patterns. You should not be influenced by what you think you should spend in each category. That step comes later and is only effective if you begin with an accurate record of how you actually use your money.

As you look over the categories, you will notice that most of them appear to be self-explanatory. Nevertheless, the following comments may be useful.

Sources of Income

Income taxed according to an employee or passive owner status includes all income you receive where you take no risk for perpetuating an organization. This includes people who work for large manufacturing corporations, service organizations, insurance companies, banks, as well as the government. This income is viewed by the taxing laws as being less worthy of work-related deductible expenses than work related expenses as a self-employed person. Thus the income taxed according to employee status is less valuable than entrepreneurial income.

Our tax laws suggest that our civilization has come full circle to medieval times. It is possible to view employees as modern serfs who may be considered to carry the major burden of government programs. Entrepreneurs would be the modern day knights who are exempt from an important part of the royalty payments to the ruling class. Persons who have tax-exempt income, such as welfare recipients, would be the equivalent of the church padres, who received only a modest income, were officially required to lead highly structured lives (but really didn't), and lived quite comfortably. Today, looking back at medieval Europe, many people would pity the serfs, yet a large number of these people are in the modern serf category. A postscript to this comparison is that the structure of medieval Europe broke down with the development of tax-free cities, which were largely populated by serfs who escaped from the manorial system.

Wages and salaries, shown on a W-2 form from the Internal Revenue Service, include all income that is derived from employers. Copies of this income are filed separately with the Internal Revenue Service, and almost all W-2 forms which have been filed with the tax authorities are routinely checked against the tax forms you file.

Interest income includes the interest you receive from savings accounts, certificates of deposit, United States Treasury securities, interest from taxable bonds, interest from mortgages you hold on other people's property, and interest from debts other people owe you.

Dividend income includes regular dividends for corporate stock. There is a federal tax exclusion for the first $200 of dividends, and federal taxes are paid on dividends over this amount. Thus, if you hold a relatively few shares of stock, typically fewer than 300 shares, dividend income is tax free. But since this exclusion is small and the tax rate after the exclusion is similar to regular employee income, dividend income is included in this part of the income statement. Pension income includes all income from company pension programs, annuities, and Social Security. The Internal Revenue Service has a record of all of the above sources of income and routinely matches your filing of income in your tax form against their records.

Other income includes that income you have received that does not involve records which have been filed with the Internal Revenue Service. Examples of this type of income include tips, work as a domestic homemaker, babysitting, the swap of dentist's services for accounting services, and honorariums for consulting, to name a few. The Internal Revenue Service relies on your honesty in reporting this income.

The second major category of income is income that is taxed according to entrepreneur status. The first type of income as an entrepreneur includes income from a proprietary business or as a director of a corporation. The expenses that may be charged against this type of income and the tax shelters that are available provide major reductions to income which are not available to persons receiving income in the employee status. Thus income received in an entrepreneur status is worth more than the same level of income received in an employee status.

For example, a person can be employed either as a tax consultant working for a corporation or as an independent, incorporated tax consultant. Both positions might be comparable in regard to gross income and most other respects. But the difference in deductions and tax savings are enormous. The independent person can deduct the business portion of his automobile cost (the employed person's commute is not deductible). Also, the independent person can deduct a portion of his or her home used in business, trips for conventions related to business, calculators and magazines used in the business, and lunches, dinners and entertaining that are business related, as well as a pension program. None of these expenses ordinarily is tax deductible as an employee.

You cannot assume that, because a corporation provides many of these benefits in some form, they are comparable to those of a personal business. For example, many employees mistakenly believe that their pension programs are comparable to the fully funded programs available to self-employed persons. Most are not comparable, since they offer vesting only after many years (when an employee has rights to a pension), few are fully funded, and many are inadequately funded (when too little money is actually placed in a pension program to back up promises). The difference between these types of programs can be large.

One friend, who was the number-two man in rank at a major corporation, was fired two months prior to his fifty-fifth birthday. At that time, his pension rights would have become vested. Those two months meant the difference between receiving an annual pension in excess of tens of thousands of dollars and not being entitled to receive any pension at all from the company. A portion of the corporation's profits had been put aside in an actuarially determined pool of funds for this executive's potential use, and presumably his salary was somewhat lower than it would have been if the corporation did not have a pension program. Nevertheless, this executive was entitled to none of the pension contributions that had been made on his behalf. If he had responsibility for his own pension, he could still have been fired, but his pension assets would have been his personal property, and he would have retained them.

Employee stock-ownership plans, which provide a way of turning employees into owners of a business, are also a part of income under the entrepreneurial category. These plans provide for the accelerated buildup of equity through various types of tax exemptions. The plans represent one of the most interesting new ideas on the business scene since the New Deal. They affect taxes as well as management, and will likely become much more important in the future.

The tax laws favor entrepreneurs over employees. Perhaps this reflects the fact that our tax laws have been written by people who are mostly proprietors and professional people and who understand the problems of this group. Perhaps it reflects a belief in individualism which is deeply rooted in this country. This belief likes to reward entrepreneur talents, or at least offset the greater risks of being responsible for a business than being hired as an employee. Thus entrepreneurial income, in this view, should be treated differently for tax purposes and considered separately in life-cycle planning.

Capital gains and losses from the sale of assets are also taxed in a way favoring this type of entrepreneurial activity. If these assets are held for more than one year, in most cases, the tax rate for the gain in value of the asset is 40 percent that of regular income. The tax laws reflect the belief in the United States that investments are good for the nation and should be encouraged.

The third category of income includes that which is tax deferred, taxed at a low rate, or not taxed at all. This group includes income where tax laws provide exceptions, as well as income that the tax laws have difficulty enforcing.

Gifts provide one type of transfer of money or assets that is either not taxed or is taxed at a relatively low rate. Inheritances, which are a type of gift, are either not taxed if they are small or are taxed at a rate considerably below that of a comparable level of income. Inheritances may involve trusts, which represent the most intricate and elevated form of the anti-tax art. Despite their complexity, these arrangements to minimize taxes are designed to preserve relationships among families and thus preserve that institution. Of course, gifts are conferred and are not earned in the same sense that income is earned. Nevertheless, the after-tax income effect of gifts to a recipient is the same as that of earned income.

Tax shelters represent income in which the tax has been deferred. These shelters may also provide a way of obtaining certain benefits from investment tax credits, and in certain instances the benefits are leveraged through borrowing. The investment tax credit provides tax reductions for certain kinds of capital spending, and it is intended to promote investment. Tax shelters represent a hybrid of tax regulations. They were developed to enable persons who have high current income to defer their tax liability until some future time. Usually, the tax liability is not eliminated—it is simply deferred. But there are times when that deferral may be important.

The Internal Revenue Service has been particularly unhappy with tax shelters and has done all in its power to enforce their provisions in a strict manner. Congress has also changed the format of these shelters, so that they no longer are as liberal in their provisions as they once were.

A third type of income that has favored tax treatment is tax-exempt securities, including municipal securities and other securities that are exempt from federal taxes. Many of these securities are exempt from state and local taxes, too, if the holder of the securities is filing a personal tax return within the locality issuing the securities. These securities are tax-exempt on the basis that governmental entities, such as the national and state governments, cannot tax each other. The tax-exempt status for state and municipal securities represents a subsidy to these governments, and it is currently believed that this subsidy helps the nation. The subsidy is the ability to issue securities to the public at a lower rate of interest than the securities would require if recipients had to pay a full tax on their income. For persons who possess sizeable wealth, the tax-exempt status of this income can be valuable.

Another category of income that is not taxed includes income noted above for which W-2 forms are not sent to the Internal Revenue Service and income that is not reported. Studies indicate that the practice of non-reported income may amount to at least 5 percent of gross national product, or nearly $150 billion annually. As taxes have grown to a larger proportion of personal income, the incentives for this form of tax evasion also have grown. Nevertheless, the risks and penalties of this practice are great. A clear record is a precious personal asset, and there are more than enough ways to achieve personal development or high income that are within the law.

Expenses

The expenses of a personal budget are divided into four categories—personal consumption, personal development, savings additions, and public consumption. These categories include expenses needed to sustain and to develop yourself, provision to build your surplus and capital, and finally, expenses in the form of taxes the government requires from you.

Personal consumption expenses include the costs of staying alive and cover the traditional expenses of food, clothing, and shelter. Housing operations include utilities and the upkeep of a home. Public transportation and auto operations include bus fare and such expenditures as interest payments on the purchase of a car, auto insurance, gas, oil, and other products used in the operation of an automobile.

These include all expenses associated with transportation, but they do not include the capital commitments of an auto purchase. Insurance in this category includes pure life insurance protection only and does not include the buildup of equity in an insurance policy, which is an addition to savings. Personal expenses include such items as haircuts, lipstick, and shoeshines. Entertainment includes movies, theater, shows, and television sets.

Personal development includes activities that have the possibility of improving your awareness of yourself, your environment, or increasing your income. These expenses represent your investment in yourself. Formal education includes attendance and courses taken at a college, university or other educational institution. Skills development includes expenses associated with the learning of a new skill on an apprenticeship basis, such as learning to fly an airplane. Reconnaissance expenses include costs associated with developing new information about your interests. For example, a canvas painter might wish to develop further information about the techniques and the market for china painting, and these expenses would be shown here. Expenses for books and literature include costs for printed matter.

Included in additions to savings are purchases of investments. These items include all funds not immediately consumed, but which are put aside to serve as a financial investment.

This third portion of a personal income statement should be looked at in the same light as corporations view their profits. It is the money you have left after you have made provisions for your bills. One way of comparing your personal profit performance would be the ratio of savings to income, just as corporations measure profitability by the ratio of profit to sales. A checking account and savings account represent typical types of savings. Purchases of stocks and bonds are common investments. The purchase of a home represents the largest and most important single investment in the savings of most people. Home ownership includes costs of basic maintenance on the structure such as roof repairs, new wiring, and painting and decorating. Maintenance costs are included as an offset to depreciation, so the physical condition of the house is maintained on a steady basis. Any change in value of the house would represent an addition to savings (when the value of the house rises) or a dissavings (if its value should drop). Other real estate, which includes purchases of apartment buildings or other houses, is handled in a similar manner.

Automobile ownership expense represents a major investment for many people, and is also treated as an asset that changes in value. Other vehicles, including recreational vehicles and motorcycles, are included here, as well as purchases of boats, gliders, or airplanes. Noninterest expense of automobiles or other vehicles that are leased are included here, since this expense includes payments for capital consumption. Purchases of other investments that are not consumed and are purchased with an intent to preserve or enhance the value of money are also shown here. Gold, silver, or diamonds are examples of these types of investments.

The final category of expenses includes those used for public consumption. These are taxes and quasi-taxes. The federal income tax is the major tax for most people. Social Security contributions are technically not a tax but a transfer payment between workers and recipients. Nevertheless, the effect of these transfer payments is the same as that of a tax. State and local taxes have become a way of life for most people, as local governments have turned to taxing income as a way of paying for their rising costs. Real estate taxes represent another common tax many people pay.

Typical Income Patterns

The second table in this chapter shows the monthly spending patterns of a typical family. It is based on the expenditures of all urban consumers as reported by the U.S. Department of Labor for December 1977. Since this government report does not take into account taxes, savings, or life insurance, the data of the report have been adjusted to show the effects of savings, a total tax rate of 19.5 percent and an insurance purchase of 1.4 percent of income. These adjustments are in line with overall population averages and may be considered to be the average spending pattern of a middle-class family in 1977. Savings rates based on national income accounts do not include these adjustments, and are much lower.

This average pattern of personal spending is not always a typical pattern in any individual case. The spending profile of a particular person often varies widely from the average shown here. Moreover, average spending patterns have changed since 1977. As everybody is well aware, petroleum prices have increased sharply, pushing gasoline costs up. At the same time, prices of household appliances have increased more slowly. Nevertheless, the spending profile of the typical person illustrates several key patterns.

The average person spends only a little more than 1 percent, or about $18 per month in 1977, for personal development. That is a small amount. Spending for entertainment is more than twice as large. Yet spending for personal development is the most critical area of spending so far as your future is concerned. In an average budget it is virtually neglected.

Another observation is that most people make sizeable additions to their savings, despite the low rate of savings of financial assets shown in gross national product data. The savings rate for those assets used here of slightly more than 6 percent is divided between checking accounts, savings accounts, and securities. This amounts to the same level as the purchase of an automobile, and it is about the same as the equity contribution to the purchase of a home. Automobile and home purchases should be considered to be part of your savings, since the buildup of equity in them is a form of savings.

There is considerable room for flexibility in the category of personal consumption. It includes the largest part of expenditures of the seven budget groups. This category can be a source of funds for other spending purposes. Similarly, an increase in income can be absorbed almost without notice in personal consumption. Often an increase in income is so quickly diverted to personal consumption that the effect of the higher income is not clearly perceived. Nevertheless, the ability to control this category of spending is perhaps the most important key to controlling your total budget.

Total taxes are not levied by a central taxing authority and are seldom looked at in total. One consequence of this is that taxes represent a larger portion of income than might be assumed by looking at taxes one at a time. Recently, the public's perception of taxes has become more acute, and the steadily growing proportion of a personal budget taken by taxes may have reached a resistance level. Nevertheless, direct taxes represented about one-fifth of the average person's income in 1977, and in 1980 that proportion was considerably higher. Taxes are another important area to search for ways to free income for other uses.

Persons with a higher income initially have a larger proportion of taxes than the average, because of progressively higher tax rates as income rises. Some of these people pay more in taxes than they spend for personal consumption. These people have a clear incentive to review their taxes carefully. Many of these people have become knowledgeable about tax-minimizing methods, but relatively few people have looked at the implications of rising taxes as one of the key factors determining the way that they perform their work.

HOW TO PREPARE YOUR BALANCE SHEET

The third table shows a balance sheet. No personal financial profile is complete without a balance sheet, and its basic purpose is to show your net worth. Your net worth is simply the total of all assets, or money, that you possess after all of your assets are added together and claims for payment against those assets are subtracted. Your net worth is perhaps more important as a measure of your financial performance than your total earnings, because it shows the cumulated results of how well you have managed your money over your lifetime.

A balance sheet is critically important if you are an entrepreneur. It measures your ability to expand the scope of your activities, and it determines how you are able to conduct your business. In contrast, if you are an employee, you don't need a balance sheet in your work, although you will need to prepare one if you plan to borrow large amounts of money for a home or a personal line of credit. But an employee's balance sheet has other purposes for your financial planning, especially if you ever intend to start your own business.

Assets

Assets include anything you own that has value. The balance sheet shown here lists five categories of assets. The top categories of assets are the most liquid, which means that they are easily converted into cash. Stocks of companies that are traded on the New York Stock Exchange are relatively liquid assets. In contrast, paintings are not frequently traded, and markets for paintings are not well organized. Thus paintings are relatively less liquid. Liquidity represents one of the key controls of your financial profile, as is discussed later.

Cash, which includes currency and coins, is the most liquid asset of all. It is the measure against which all other assets are compared when their liquidity is evaluated. Cash is capable of almost instant conversion into almost any other asset. The holder of sufficient cash may, within a matter of hours, buy a house, bonds, or perhaps even a Rembrandt painting. The drawback of cash is that it earns no interest. Thus the penalty for having instant convertibility to any other asset—which cash possesses—is a loss of earning power. Checking accounts are close substitutes for cash. Nevertheless, even NOW checking accounts earn relatively little interest on a net basis. These accounts are a type of checking account that either earns interest on your balance, or offsets checking account charges by the amount of your balance.

Time deposits earn interest, and the amount that they earn is in proportion to their liquidity. For example, deposits in passbook savings accounts may be withdrawn virtually whenever the bank, savings and loan, or other financial institution is open. If the savings deposit is left with the financial institution for a period of time, it will earn a higher rate of interest. The period of time is pre-arranged at the time of deposit, and a longer period of deposit brings a higher interest rate. You cannot withdraw funds prior to the agreed-on time without paying a penalty.

The cash surrender value of life insurance is a highly liquid asset, and the cash value of an annuity policy is also liquid. These insurance policies consist of insurance that will be paid upon the death of the insured, and they accumulate equity benefits much like a savings account. If you wish to use these funds, technically you do not withdraw money from an insurance company, rather you borrow against the accumulated assets and pay an interest charge. The interest rate is usually considerably lower than the cost of borrowing. It is usually not as convenient to use the accumulated equity benefits of an insurance policy as it is to withdraw a savings account. Insurance companies require an exchange of correspondence with the head office of the insurance company. Despite these inconveniences and technicalities, equity benefits of an insurance policy should be regarded as an important source of liquidity.

Automobiles and other vehicles are another type of highly liquid asset which many people own. Automobiles are highly liquid, because there is a market for their sale virtually everywhere. Even small towns usually include at least one used-car dealer who will buy a car instantly. Most people do not consider their automobile as an asset, because they use their car in their daily living. Nevertheless, there are usually, but not always, alternatives to a car, such as public transportation or a car pool. In addition, you could usually sell or trade your car for a less expensive model and in so doing liquidate part of your automobile asset. Another reason most people do not consider their automobile to be a liquid asset is that they don't want to be reminded that this asset usually depreciates rapidly.

Money owed you and checks yet to arrive are another type of liquid asset. Although forthcoming checks may never arrive, particularly if the remitting person never intends to send them, in most instances checks in transit will arrive and represent a liquid asset. Sometimes the check will require clearance and payment by the remitting bank before you have use of the funds. Sometimes checks are not good. Thus all checks may require a delay of several days before you have the use of funds and are not as liquid as cash or a savings account. Nevertheless, compared with all types of assets, checks should be regarded as being liquid assets.

Money-market securities are becoming a common type of liquid asset. These securities include U.S. Treasury bills, negotiable certificates of deposit, and shares in money-market funds that pass through interest to shareholders. Money-market securities are short-term debt instruments, with a maturity of less than one year. There is an active market for most of these securities, and they may be bought or sold quickly and easily, usually within a matter of minutes if you are known to a general securities broker or to a bank's trading desk. Otherwise, you will need to visit the offices of one of these organizations, identify yourself, and provide basic financial information about yourself.

Money-market instruments are bought and sold in relatively large amounts. U.S. Treasury bills are sold in minimum denominations of $10,000, commercial paper $25,000, and negotiable certificates of deposit $100,000. Nevertheless, some money market funds accept minimum amounts of $1,000 or less. Many of these funds offer a way of redeeming your assets by providing bank drafts which may be used like a check for amounts of $500 or more.

Notes and bonds are similar to money-market instruments, except that they mature in a period longer than one year and interest is paid in regular installments. Notes usually mature within seven years, and bonds mature seven years or longer from the date of issuance. Most notes and bonds from major borrowers, such as the United States government, major utilities, and corporations, are frequently traded and can be bought and sold quickly. Prices of major bonds and notes are quoted daily in the *Wall Street Journal.* They are traded by most general securities brokers, and government bonds are traded by large banks. Most bonds are issued in denominations of $1,000 or larger.

Notes and bonds are not quite as liquid as money-market securities, but the difference in liquidity is not usually very significant. In addition, the price of bonds may fluctuate considerably more than the price of money-market instruments.

Stocks of companies listed on the New York Stock Exchange or the American Exchange are also liquid, since both exchanges provide a specialist for each listed stock. The job of the specialist is to provide an orderly market for a stock. Major over-the-counter (OTC) stocks also are liquid. Any of these stocks usually can be sold for cash quickly and easily.

Gold and the principal other precious metals—silver and platinum—are relatively liquid. Most of these metals are in coin or an ingot with an assay mark. In either case, the value may be quickly determined. In recent years the trading market for these metals has rapidly developed, and there are now traders in virtually every city.

The total of these various types of assets is your liquid asset position. This total represents the amount of cash you could raise within one day by the sale of these assets.

The second category of assets are those that are relatively illiquid. If these assets were sold for cash, it would ordinarily require more than one day to sell them. In some instances it could take a year or longer to find a buyer and complete a sale.

Mortgages are one type of relatively illiquid asset. Nevertheless, in commercial centers, mortgages often may be sold within a few days. First mortgages are more liquid than second mortgages. When a sale is required, these assets are typically sold to other private parties, although they may be sold to financial institutions. Debts of relatives and friends are illiquid assets, since it is difficult to find somebody who would want to buy them. Letter stock is also an illiquid asset since this stock cannot be sold to anyone other than the issuing corporation.

Property investments are probably the most illiquid assets of all. The sale of even the most desirable property requires several weeks to complete before you can receive cash payment. Homes are usually the quickest type of property to sell, while apartment buildings and commercial properties often require a longer period of time to sell. Undeveloped land is usually the most illiquid type of property.

Paintings and objects of art are illiquid assets, because it is usually difficult to assess their value and find a buyer. Diamonds and precious gems are relatively illiquid except at a discount, unless you live in New York, London, Antwerp, or Hong Kong, which are centers for wholesale diamond merchants. Collector stamps may be sold to local stamp dealers, but to be assured of a correct price, you would probably want to submit stamps to one of the major national trading houses. Unless you happen to live in one of the cities where these houses are located, there would be a delay in making a sale while the stamps were shipped.

Most other assets would also require a delay of a week or longer before you could receive cash payment. These assets include antiques, planes, and boats.

Liabilities

Liabilities include all promises of payment that you have made. Most financial reports separate liabilities into those due within one year, but a personal budget typically operates on a much shorter time span than a corporation. Thus the balance sheet shown here divides liabilities into a category of those debts due within one month and debts due in a longer period ahead. Moreover, most personal debt is amortized, meaning that even relatively small personal debts are broken down into regular, scheduled monthly payments.

Current liabilities include notes payable within 30 days and charge accounts and bills payable within 30 days. It also includes money presently due to friends and relatives. The current monthly mortgage payments and current second-mortgage payments are also part of current liabilities.

Long-term liabilities include the portion of debt that remains beyond 30 days. First and second mortgages less the current monthly payment, as well as the unpaid portion of notes and other obligations are also long-term liabilities. Income taxes due above the amount withheld represent another long-term liability.

Net Worth

The total of all assets less liabilities shows your net worth, and it is the last item of your balance sheet. I have always been fascinated with the concept of net worth. It is truly the heart of a financial profile, since it represents the ultimate purpose of every other financial activity. Increasing your income, controlling expenses, buying and selling assets, acquiring debt and paying it off are all activities that aim to accomplish the one final purpose of enhancing net worth. And yet, despite its importance, net worth cannot be directly controlled. It is really a residual. It is what is left after you have put your hands to rest.

Chapter 4

YOUR FOUR KEY MONEY CONTROLS

*C*ONTROL is perhaps the most unpopular word in any language. It suggests restriction. Most organization charts in companies are control diagrams, indicating that certain people are managed or controlled by other people. All people in the organization chart who lie below the top are restricted, since those who are placed lower in the chart ordinarily do not carry on discussions with persons who are located higher in the chart. Salesman are controlled by their customers, and they are limited in the scope of people with whom they conduct business. Most people do not like to think that their associations in business are as closely controlled as, in fact, they are. But control is an important part of business organization. It is the way a business focuses its attention on opportunities and problems. Control enables you to be selective and make decisions concerning which activities are most important.

People treat their social life in a similar manner. They focus their attention on friends who give them the most enjoyment and fun, or in some cases, the most prestige. Very few people are indiscriminately friendly with everybody they meet. Control is an important part of each day in our lives.

External controls are only part of the way we order our lives. There are more important internal controls. Internal controls are the directions we take because we believe that they are correct for us. They are signals which we use for guidance that have not been forced on us. By voluntarily selecting these internal controls, we do not resent them. If we should believe that certain internal controls are no longer correct, we can freely change them. Examples of internal controls are treating strangers on the street with common courtesy and giving money to a worthy cause because we believe in the work it represents. Nobody forces us to do these things, but they reflect the way we see ourselves.

WHY YOU NEED MONEY CONTROLS

Managing money involves the use of internal controls. If you consider yourself to be a manager of money rather then simply a spender of money, you are responding to internal controls. Internal controls are a result of a decision to concentrate our efforts and simplify our lives. When we set our sights on certain objectives and decide to use controls to help us accomplish those objectives, we automatically reduce the number of decisions we need to make. Our financial controls give us a quick reading of how to use our money. Controls are a powerful tool. They remind us of our objectives whenever we use our money.

There are four financial controls you need to manage your money: (1) savings rate, (2) liquidity, (3) leverage, and (4) incremental tax rate. If you know where you stand with each of these financial controls and understand their implications, you will be able to direct the financial part of your life effectively.

SAVINGS RATE

The total expenditures of a budget are divided into three broad parts, as shown in the previous chapter. The first part is personal consumption and includes living expenses and personal development expenses. Taxes represent a second part, and the third part is savings, which includes the portion of income that is not consumed or taxed.

The savings rate is calculated by dividing savings by total income. For example, if a person saved $75 per month and had a total income of $1,500 per month, the person's savings rate would be 5 percent, or $75 divided by $1,500 times 100.

You should save approximately 20 percent of your income throughout your life cycle. That rate represents a somewhat higher rate than the average for a typical person noted in the previous chapter. A 20 percent savings rate is not a difficult target to achieve, but it usually requires some planning.

There will be times in your life cycle when you will take on large debt, such as when you buy a house, and there will be times in your life when you will spend money more liberally for personal development. All of these changes in your pattern of consumption are useful, and your savings rate will fluctuate during these periods.

For example, when you buy a house, your consumption expenses will increase. If you move from an apartment to a house, the move will shift monthly rental payments from a living expense to an investment expense, and the latter is a savings category. But the move also places a strain on the budget through unusual or extraordinary expenses. Moving costs, redecorating, new furniture, and various repairs and modifications to a house always seem to swamp the budget of everybody who moves. Most people also incur many of these expenses when they move from one rental home to another.

Nevertheless, a good money manager sets a limit to the total expense a move should involve and pares back the remainder of the budget so that other consumption expenses are reduced for several months. It takes considerable restraint, but the effort is worthwhile.

A personal experience showed me that this type of restraint is useful. The first house we bought had a light green carpet in the living room, and my wife and I agreed that we should replace it with a tan carpet as soon as possible. We obtained an estimate for the new carpet and felt that we couldn't afford the expense at the time we moved in. We eventually lived with that carpet until we sold the house. We recognized that the color of the carpet had been selected by the previous owners to reflect the countryside which spread before the windows. We had initially only looked at the room as a box with four walls and had looked at the wood paneling as the key color. Our restraint on spending gave us the time which was necessary to properly evaluate the living room, and we were glad that we did not replace the carpet.

The purchase of a car usually adds to consumption expenses, since people who buy a new car usually drive more and increase their costs of transportation. Illness represents another way that consumption expenses can rise, often quickly. Nevertheless, there are usually long periods of many months, or even several years, when consumption expenses are not under pressure. During these more stable periods, your savings rate should be somewhat above your long-term average, in order to even out the periods when your savings rate will fall below that level.

A budget can be viewed as a tug-of-war between savings and consumption. Income that is not consumed or taxed is saved. It is usually more pleasant to consume income than it is to save income, although there are exceptions. For example, many people think of their home as a pleasant way of adding to savings. Nevertheless, most savings and investments do not involve personal use and require the belief that they have merit and value, even if they cannot be enjoyed.

To increase your savings rate, reduce your consumption or tax rate. Of course, an increase in income can permit you to increase your consumption and not bring about a change in the amount of money allocated for savings. However, in this instance the savings rate would decline. The key is to keep the savings rate steady so that an increase in income will benefit savings proportionately. Your savings rate may rise as your income increases. A person receiving a high income tends to be able to afford all of his or her necessities and has more income available for savings. Yet the irony of this observation is that the necessity for savings tends to increase as income declines. People with low incomes have a greater need to increase savings, because the proper use of savings represents an important vehicle to improve their income. Whatever your income, savings represents the means to develop yourself, and that need remains almost the same throughout your life and changes in your income level.

Most people find that the most difficult time they face to keep their savings rate intact is during the period immediately following a large increase in income. A sudden raise has a heady effect, and most people loosen their budget to enjoy the good fortune. In a burst of celebration, spending can often become larger than the increased income. In these cases, a raise can be the worst thing that can happen to a budget. Nevertheless, after a brief spree, most people get hold of their budget and realize that they have overindulged.

Your savings rate should be immune from the broad economic trends which surround you. Your savings portfolio may change in its composition, but the rate should remain steady regardless of what happens to the economy. For example, during the 1970s, inflation became a major issue for everybody. Many commentators spoke of the penalty savers were taking, since savings accounts paid 5 percent interest, which was less than the current rate of increase of the consumer price index. That comment was correct. Savings accounts were really being taxed by the government. The interest rate of savings accounts was regulated by the government at about 5 percent, and the difference between that rate and the inflation rate represented lost buying power. Nevertheless, the savings portion of a budget is much broader than savings accounts, and it should include additions to equity in homes, real estate, gold, and other assets. These assets have risen more rapidly than the rate of inflation in recent years.

In the future it is possible that the economy could enter a

deflationary era. Although that development is not considered likely, if it occurred the savings rate of a budget should also remain steady. Nevertheless, its composition would shift. Deflation hedges are the opposite of inflation hedges and include fixed-income securities and the ownership of mortgages. Virtually any conceivable type of economic climate would make little difference to the savings rate of a budget. The only exception would be a national catastrophe, such as widespread unemployment or a devastating war fought on the nation's homeland. Under such extreme circumstances, which many people have faced in Europe, Africa, and Asia, personal survival becomes more important than saving, and people do whatever they can to stay alive.

Some observers have suggested that during certain periods of your life you should not worry about saving, since your expenses are supposed to be high and the government will protect you from any major financial need. This advice is not sound. It is important to take on debt at various times in your life, but it is not wise to allow the size of interest expense that is needed to service this debt to become so large that it eliminates savings. Moreover, some debt is used to buy assets that typically appreciate in value such as houses, while other debt is used to buy assets that typically decline in value such as automobiles, refrigerators, stoves, and household furniture. Borrowing costs to finance those depreciating assets should not crowd out savings, except under unusual or temporary circumstances.

The key to understanding the importance of your savings rate may be to think of it in terms of its time horizon. Savings represents money that is oriented to the future, while consumption is money that is focused on the present. Savings requires a deferral of the present use of money for its future use. We need to be sustained in our daily life, and we can only live in the present, so consumption spending is essential. An overly high savings rate can lead to a life like Scrooge, which defeats the broader, human purposes of savings.

The savings rate provides you with a valuable guideline which makes you think twice about consumption habits. It is not forced upon you, as are delinquency notices or past-due debts. Your reward for taking control of your savings pattern is to give you the ability to build your net worth, and that provides you with wider opportunities for self-development than are possible from any gift, government decree, or lucky day.

LEVERAGE

The ability to use a small amount of capital to control much larger wealth is leverage. The simplest example of leverage is a home mortgage, which currently is based on a down payment of capital of 10 or 20 percent, and often a loan for the remainder for five years. At the end of that period, the remaining debt would be refinanced with a new loan. In some cases, down payments of five percent have been adequate, and I am aware of situations in which all of a down payment has been borrowed, as well as funds to take care of the initial mortgage payments. That represents the ultimate example of leverage.

The down payment of a home mortgage is a commitment of capital. The willingness of a lender to provide the difference between the down payment and the sale price reflects the confidence of a lender that the borrower will honorably pay the difference. I am always impressed by the fact that there is long-term credit for individuals. The development of widespread consumer credit and institutions that serve this credit should rank as one of the great economic achievements of our age. There has not been anything similar in history.

Leverage is a powerful tool to build net worth. It is also a powerful tool for disaster, if it is not handled carefully or if financial and business conditions turn out to be different than had been originally expected. Leverage is a double-edged sword. It can cut large assets to manageable proportions, or it can cut the hand of the holder.

Many people have not fully appreciated the risks of leverage. Commitments of large sums of money for many years into the future involve considerable risk. Often these commitments are greater than the net worth of the person who holds them. The risk is not that something could happen to the borrower. If that happened, the asset could be sold and the debt could be liquidated. The risk is that economic conditions would make the asset decline in value so that the unpaid amount would be greater than the market value of the asset. That situation has not happened very often and is brushed aside by most current commentators. We are often assured that the momentum of the past will be continued. Nevertheless, anyone who has even a remote acquaintance with the history of credit markets or has lived more than 50 years is aware that this assurance should be viewed with a certain amount of skepticism.

There is good reason to believe that in the span of many decades, productivity will rise more rapidly than population and productivity gains will tend to reward people who use leverage. Nevertheless, during certain periods, such as depressions or periods of controls and uncertainties, it would be best not to be leveraged. But nobody is smart enough to know when these difficult periods will occur, especially when leverage commitments often extend 20 to 30 years into the future.

Moreover, periods of severe economic distress are usually periods of difficulty in finding enough money to cover maintenance costs. Renters pay slowly, vacancies rise, and earnings are difficult to obtain. When these periods occur, a nonleveraged position is best, since you have unimpaired capital. Your net worth is sitting on your balance sheet without major liabilities above it. That net worth is then available to leverage assets, and you are able to leverage a much larger amount of real assets than previously.

The two edges of leverage are often overlooked during both speculative booms and periods of difficulty. For example, I recall attending a wedding party in New York in the summer of 1968, the last year of the great bull market of the

1960s. It was almost impossible to talk about anything other than the stock market. People who had never looked at a corporate balance sheet, never looked at the products nor the customers of a company, passed what they believed was inside information to each other. Moreover, most of the companies being disussed were secondary stocks and were small organizations that had never experienced a difficult business environment. I had the feeling that what I heard must have been characteristic of the late 1920s. There was one important exception—during the 1920s it was possible to leverage a stock by placing only 10 percent of funds against the total purchase price of the stock. The remainder was borrowed. In 1968 stocks were only slightly leveraged, with approximately two-thirds of the purchase price required for payment. The subsequent two-year decline in the price of secondary stocks, which was much more severe than the decline in the Dow Jones average, did not have the devastating effect on stock holders as the declines of 1929 and 1932.

The changes in economic conditions represent important limits to your use of leverage. You do not want to expose yourself to a loss of your assets, as could happen if you were to be highly leveraged and a deep recession and a deflation were to occur. On the other hand, avoiding leverage during an upsweep in business conditions and an acceleration in the rate of inflation can represent lost opportunities.

These are limits, not strategies. Your purpose is not to outguess financial markets, which only a very few people have done successfully over the years. You should use leverage at various stages of your life cycle, and at other stages you should avoid leverage. The decision of whether you should use leverage should be determined, first of all, by your personal needs and your stage of the life cycle. The second consideration is the soundness of the business opportunity and your appraisal of future business conditions.

The decision to link your use of leverage to your life cycle is not easy to accept. Markets can become quite strong, and at times it would appear that you would be missing financial opportunities. It is true that at certain times you might be missing an opportunity to increase your net worth. But leveraged transactions are very time consuming, because their risk requires frequent monitoring. During certain periods of your life cycle, such as the midlife challenge, you should avoid the additional stress and risk of leverage. At those times, your main concern is your personal development. It would be a mistake to trade further steps in your personal development, which also require time and effort, for an addition to your net worth, no matter how large that addition potentially might be. Without the additional insight into your interests and goals, you would not be able to use the additional money to its full advantage. It would be better to have less money and a better grasp of yourself. Then, during the succeeding years of your life cycle, you can turn to leverage and use it to your full potential.

LIQUIDITY

As mentioned previously, your balance sheet consists of various types of assets, some of which are readily convertible to cash. These liquid assets include checking accounts and savings accounts, since you can quickly turn the entire amount of these accounts into cash. Illiquid assets include assets that require time or some amount of difficulty to convert into cash. Vacant land is a common illiquid asset, since its sale usually requires a considerable amount of time to find a buyer. Moreover, once a buyer places a bid for the land and the bid is accepted, time is required to authenticate and transfer the title. When you do receive payment, it may be in an out-of-state check, and your bank may not release funds to you until the check clears, which could involve more time. Typically, several months may elapse between the time you decide to sell the property and the time you receive cash. Most other forms of savings lie between these two extremes of liquid and illiquid assets.

The balance sheet you prepared in the previous chapter divides your assets into the two broad categories of liquid and illiquid assets. Of course, there may be exceptions to this classification. For example, under the category of illiquid assets you may own a particularly famous painting for which a museum has offered you a sizeable sum, and you need only present the painting to receive payment. Or a friend may have found a better-paying job and be able to make payment on the note he gave you. But exceptions are likely to be few. Most of the assets under the illiquid category would require some time to convert into cash.

Both liquid and illiquid assets have their place in your investment program. During periods of your life cycle when you expect rapid change, you should add liquid assets. For example, during your adolescent stage you will be developing your personal identity and exploring your talents and skills at work. Your financial needs may change rapidly, as you become aware of a new skill you might wish to explore. You might develop an interest in carpentry and wish to buy expensive wood-working tools. The ability to buy tools quickly would reflect your liquidity or credit standing.

In another example, you might be in the period of age and simplicity. This is also a period of exploration, and the format for development is likely to be inward, perhaps religious. You may wish to attend a series of lectures or visit a location that has developed particular significance for you. Your liquidity would give you the means to follow that interest without delay.

These examples show that liquid assets have the advantage of giving flexibility to your activities. Liquidity gives you the financial ability to adapt to changes in your life and interests. It frees you. It does not tie you to long-standing commitments.

However, liquidity is costly. In many cases, liquid assets you hold will show a lower rate of interest or appreciation than illiquid assets. This relationship does not apply to all situations, but it is common enough to serve as a general rule. The most common example of the cost of liquidity is shown by the schedule of interest rates that banks and thrift institutions pay. Regular passbook savings pay the lowest interest rate. If you agree to deposit your money for three months, you will receive a higher rate of interest. A year for your deposit brings a higher rate, and if you agree to leave your money in the institution for several years, you will often receive an interest rate that is double that of a passbook savings account.

During periods of your life cycle when you will not be expecting change, you will not need to pay a premium for liquidity. During these periods, your stability will enable you to give preference to illiquid assets. You would then collect the extra financial benefits that illiquidity provides.

For example, during the adult stage you may wish to purchase a home. You may also make other purchases of real estate during this period. The personal stability of the period provides a certainty of your continued interest in these leveraged purchases.

INCREMENTAL TAX RATE

In an era of rising inflation, such as has occurred during the decade of the 1970s, almost every person under the age of 30 may face important career issues, unless the trend of rising incremental tax rates is stopped and reversed. This situation involves more than one-half of the nation's population. No other financial issue seems destined to become a matter of such overriding importance.

Your incremental tax rate is the rate of tax you pay on each additional dollar that you earn. The United States federal income tax and most state and local taxes rise more rapidly than your income rises. This characteristic is often described as a "progressive" tax rate. This means that as you earn more, you will pay even more tax.

Many people compare the taxes that they pay with their total income in order to determine their tax position. That is a mistake. In a progressive tax program, such as you face, your average tax rate will always be smaller than your incremental tax rate. The average tax rate does not accurately convey the seriousness of your tax problems until it becomes acute. Thus you may miss important financial decisions, if you are not aware of the tax implications of your current situation.

The tax laws clearly favor people who are in business for themselves and give them advantages that are not available to people who work as employees. This difference reflects a preference toward being in business for yourself. The nation's lawmakers, in Congress, state legislatures, and in city councils, tend to be independent lawyers, insurance agents, shopkeepers, farmers, and businesspeople. Many lawmakers who write tax laws believe that these independent businesspeople are the backbone of the nation. They know that being in business for yourself takes risk and a greater amount of self-discipline than is usually required of employees, and that these values should be encouraged.

The attitude of government toward taxes involves another implication. The theoretical basis of a progressive tax structure is that there should be a redistribution of income from the wealthy to the poor. However, in recent years there actually has been a distribution of income from the middle class to the poor. The rich have been able to protect themselves from taxes. These persons are usually not employees. They are proprietors, owners, or professional people who are able to arrange their business affairs so that they are taxed according to business or corporate tax rules, which include liberal deductions and lower tax rates.

One of your important career questions is whether you should work as an employee or start your own business or business group. In considering this question, preferences are important. Some people could never be happy as an employee, and other people could never endure life as an entrepreneur. But most people do not fit into one of those extreme molds. Most people could function quite well either as an employee or as an independent business person. Most people are adaptable enough to function well in either situation.

If personal issues are not critical, tax issues could be very important to whether you should work as an employee or employer. In fact, unless you are one of the relatively few persons who would be comfortable only as an employee, you should be an employee for one of two reasons. You should be an employee if you have reached a high corporate or government position and enjoy the feeling of power over other people which accompanies that position. There is no question that political power, which a high government or corporate position gives, can be satisfying in this respect. As a guideline, your income should be in the top 20 percent of your age group in your government or corporate position in order for you to pursue this type of career. If you are in a more subordinate level and if you cannot find such a higher position in another company or governmental unit, you should consider a business of your own. The other reason you may wish work as an employee is that you may be using your employer as a source of capital to fund a future enterprise.

There are two periods of your life cycle when you may be most motivated to start your own business. These pressures are strongest during adolescence and the midlife challenge. During those periods you will find your relationship to your work to be more searching than during other periods.

There is, of course, an alternative to a rising incremental tax rate. That is the alternative of leisure. Most people who have worked long hours and are dedicated to their work would reject this alternative emotionally without further thought. Yet the alternative is logical and reasonable.

Leisure can be as satisfying and challenging as work. In fact, both are essential to a balanced, long-term view of your life. Leisure does not mean that you do nothing. Leisure means that you pursue activities which are enjoyable and stimulating to you without any significant financial rewards. Leisure activities do not involve deadlines or profit-and-loss statements, but they do require personal satisfaction. If you have reached a level of income that takes care of your needs and a progressive tax rate gives you lessening rewards for your added effort, more leisure can make sense.

The beat generation, flower children, and hippies were sending this message to the working people in the past. These people carried the idea of leisure to an extreme, and most people were shocked by their apparent indifference and laziness. Yet, they showed that there were limits to hard work, and that if you reached these limits, you had, in fact, "arrived." Further work then would be nonproductive in terms of your personal utility and use of time.

When I began working, none of my friends had doubts about the eventual success of their careers or the future of the organizations that they worked for. They believed that more work would bring more recognition, which would bring more benefits and more money. All of this is changing. I recently spoke to a group of the leading graduate schools of business on the subject of future trends in financial institutions. I was unprepared for questions which asked how people could control their working environment. I asked the group why they wanted to control their working environment. Several of these young people said that this was the only way to freedom in modern life, since high positions as employees brought high taxes, and you could find yourself employed by a corporation but working for the government.

It is my belief that no one should earn over $70,000 as an employee. There is no financial purpose to this, only the desire for power or image. Earnings above $70,000 as an employee, after allowance for typical deductions and adjustments, usually involve being in a combined federal and state (where applicable) incremental tax bracket that is higher than 50 percent. That means that extra earnings represent a transfer to the government of money which is greater than your reward for your work. If you do earn more than $70,000 as an employee, you should be more concerned about your deductions than increasing your earnings.

This sounds terrible to most people who were brought up to think of being increasingly more useful and productive. Deductions give an impression of being more concerned about cutting corners than being productive. That isn't so. It is simply recognizing the rules of the game of making a living that have been imposed by the government. The best response is to plan your life to be able to play that game to your best advantage, all within the law. You want to be sure that your work will financially reward you as much as possible. It is better for you to arrange your work and activities so that you may keep your money, or give it to the charities of your choice than for you to be taxed in progressively higher brackets.

Incidentally, you must always handle your taxes in a completely honest manner and pay every penny you legally owe the government. There is no other policy. Your record with these authorities is important. If the government considers you to be a cheater, for whatever reason, you may be frequently audited. Audits take time to fulfill, and they are nerve-wracking experiences. You should not fear an audit if you have good records and have honestly presented your tax papers. In fact, good record keeping is the key in winning on a tax audit. Nor is it sound to prepare your taxes to try to preclude an audit at all costs, if that effort requires you to omit legitimate deductions. But in the long run, you will lose if you are not completely honest with the tax authorities.

The implications of incremental taxes in an inflationary era are enormous to anybody who is concerned about making work meaningful. Even with occasional tax cuts, the tax burden weighs ever more heavily on industrious employees. As you plan your money management and your life's activities, you will need to look at ways of minimizing your tax burden as you maximize your personal development. Tax courses, special tax tips, and tax planning have their place, and are important. But the issue is bigger than tax accounting, which is largely defensive. The basic question is how you plan and adapt your life in view of the tax laws.

PART III
STAGES OF MONEY IN THE LIFE CYCLE

Chapter 5

THE ADOLESCENT AWAKENING: AGE 14 TO 22

*A*DOLESCENCE is the first period when we develop a sense of ourselves. It is a period of awakening, of personal discovery, when we try to understand who we are, and direct that understanding to accomplish something.

Money management begins during adolescence because the control we choose for ourselves involves the way we manage our money. Many children manage money with apparent skill. But the skill is not really a child's choice, since money management of a child principally reflects the wishes and directions of parents or other adults.

The idea that we are a person unto ourselves, different from our parents, relatives, and friends, is a shocking realization. Our emerging sense of who we are usually challenges the ideas and patterns of life that our parents have required us to follow, and stress is not easy to live with. We want to continue patterns we feel comfortable with, and yet we are compelled to develop new directions that uniquely belong to us. The arguments, emotional scenes, the moments of despair followed by moments of elation reflect a never-ending struggle. It may appear that neither the adolescent nor parents or guardians win, but that view is mistaken. The adolescent wins through greater confidence in his or her ability to test a full range of emotions. After each encounter, the adolescent usually achieves more personal identity, and with that identity or integrating experience, more control.

During the adolescent years, the challenge to the old ways of conducting ourselves is pushed to an extreme. There will be two later periods when the challenge of old ways will again become a major preoccupation of our lives, during midlife stage and the age and simplicity stage. These later stages may be more tumultuous if adolescence is not adequately dealt with. But never again will we push ourselves with such fervor. Adolescence is our first bout with the discovery of who we are. We have little previous experience with our personal identity, and this new challenge is difficult to handle.

The destruction of our old patterns of life is not easy. They represent a great sense of security. Adolescents seldom say goodbye smoothly to their old way of living. They rush to their new identity, and tear out the old ways with a ruthlessness that gives an impression of callousness. But this is not the case. The process of coming to see oneself requires an enormous amount of personal sensitivity. Adolescents only appear callous to others. The concentration of concern to their inner self creates a focus that leaves little concern for the feelings of other people. Adolescents possess the great resources of energy so needed to reconcile the creative aspects and destructive necessities of their lives.

The purpose of the upheaval of adolescence is to forge a unique, integrated identity. When a person enters adolescence, he or she is largely a mirror of other people. When that person leaves adolescence, he or she is like no one else. The person then has a mind of his or her own, an understanding of skills and talents that are useful, and a sense of control over the emotions and ideas that are reflected by this new sense of personal identity.

The control and mastery over oneself is the successful outcome of adolescence, and it is this control which is critical to managing your money successfully. Yet the development of mastery and control which ushers in the end of the adolescent period also marks the end to the creative aspects of self-discovery. It is as if the rules of life were suspended during adolescence in order to let personal interests, strengths, and weaknesses fall where they may. The period is as close to anarchy in our personal lives as we will ever reach. It is a necessary anarchy, because if the rules of our parents were not released, we would never be able to look at ourselves as we are.

Adolescents play-act. They look at the way others act, and in the finest tradition of theater, pretend that all the world is their stage. They try each part of life as they see it, sometimes as a teacher, other times as a friend, and again as a television personality. As they try these various roles, they evaluate the part that they are playing, to determine whether they fit the role. If adolescents look ridiculous at times to other observers, they usually sense the same message.

Adolescents are their own severest critics. This self-criticism is more severe than at any other stage of the life cycle. During two later periods, midlife and age, self-criticism will again become important. But it will never likely again be as severe, or as thorough. Criticism is sometimes a destructive and at other times a constructive force. It cuts across these descriptions. Perhaps that is why we sometimes hear people say they would welcome constructive criticism, when they really mean that they would not like to hear anything which would upset their plans. Criticism is guided by observations and logic, not plans and hopes. Where criticism leads is unpredictable. It tears down in ways that cannot be foreseen. It throws out useless encumbrances. It leaves behind all the sentimental accumulations each of us builds up whenever we avoid difficult choices. In its place, we are given a few key central beliefs that tie everything together. Its simplicity gives us a renewed freedom and a new efficiency. We become stronger and more effective.

The price that is paid for undergoing a strong dose of self-criticism is a bit of inhumanity, and adolescents are not known for being tolerant of each other. No member of an adolescent group escapes criticism, and most adolescents are continually trying to adjust to some comment they interpret as criticism. They examine each piece of their being, each facet of their existence. The parts that are a reflection of their parents' wishes and are not truly part of their personal makeup are purged. It is a cutting, stressful experience.

The benefits are enormous. From the self-criticism comes a truer understanding of the hopes, needs, faith, and talents of each adolescent. If this process were not to occur, we would spend our lives in a pattern which could not change or progress. We would be slaves to our parental "scripts," and foreigners to our own talents.

Yet adolescence is also a period of idealism. The process of self-criticism has a simplifying effect, and when the despair of self-doubt gives way to hope, the ideals that are projected are simpler and clearer than life. The idealism of an adolescent is as unrealistic as is the despair. But both are part of the same logic that cuts away all details and leaves only the essential outlines of our ideas. The despair of an adolescent acts as a discouragement, and without the hope of idealism, the adolescent would soon be paralyzed.

Idealism can lead to an enthusiasm that would bring about exhaustion if it were not tempered. Learning to live with criticism and idealism, in their depth and intensity, is a challenge the adolescent gropes with daily. As these extremes are understood and controlled, the adolescent moves ahead to the next stage of the life cycle, which is adulthood. But control does not come easily. It is a result of repeated failures and successes.

The intensity of feeling of an adolescent plumbs the depths and searches the heights of his or her nature. Adolescents who have the strength to reach out the farthest also run the greatest risk of slipping into a state of mind where they cut themselves off from their family and friends. Most adolescents sense this invisible line and do not move beyond it, except for short periods of time. Wherever this line occurs, it represents the outer limits of exploration. Those who can move the farthest, endure the most self-criticism, and withstand the severest tension usually reap the greatest benefits of self-awareness. They will have traveled the farthest, sensed the most, and understood themselves the best. Thus the wildest or most difficult adolescents often turn into persons who can control themselves effectively in the adulthood stage of their life cycle. Their ability to cope with conflict reflects strength.

The saddest experience of an adolescent is not to experience the cutting edge of self-criticism and to tie oneself to the past. It is as if an invisible glass wall cuts these people from the raging conflict that lies within them. They preserve their childhood hopes, fears, and dreams. They are not shaken to the core by the realization that they are a person who cannot be a perfect fulfillment of the wishes of their parents. The price that they pay for this composure is that they cannot become more than they have been. They are frozen in time. Their potential for self-development is circumscribed.

The purpose of adolescence is to take the first giant steps toward self-development. The discovery of one's self, one's true dimensions and abilities, one's strengths and weaknesses is an exciting mission. It is all-encompassing, and it makes all other purposes of life secondary.

Nevertheless, we live in a society that makes many demands on adolescents. We demand that they attend a highly structured school system that probably is suited for the self-development of only a relative few. We demand that they participate in behavior and dress codes that are widely in use and permit change only after considerable collective protest on their part. We occasionally demand that they join in an armed force to fight other adolescents. It is remarkable that all of these demands on adolescents have relatively little effect on their ability to carry forward their self-development. It is as if adolescents sense the importance of their personal mission, keep their inner struggles intact, and accommodate the rest of society the best way they can.

The adolescent also looks to others in a new light, and progressively cuts himself or herself away from the earlier family and begins to search for a new group for identity.

Moreover, personal identity becomes interrelated with sex. Although children have a sense of gender, their sense of personal identity is not closely wrapped up with sex. The groups that adolescents form provide the first step in understanding themselves through the sharing of their close personal experiences with persons other than their families. The groups provide a reflection of their own inner experiences, and this sharing gives them confidence that they can be understood by somebody, as their families become more distant.

The groups of adolescents eventually break apart and adolescents pair, seeking someone who appears as the perfect mate. They are no longer a part of a family that has nurtured them and accepted them as they are. The adolescent now has created his or her own family, and created a new family in the way he or she wishes. The new family reflects the identity of both parties.

The sexual union reflects the union in personal identities. Both a sense of personal identity and sex appear to develop simultaneously, and each appears to require the other for fulfillment. The adolescent explores one as he or she explores the other. The development of an adolescent's sense of identity involves a growth of the ability to greatly extend intimate relationships such as friendship, love, and most of all, intimacy with oneself. It involves the coming of age of one's inner resources, extending the range of one's excitements and commitments.

Intimacy is really the ability to fuse your identity with someone else's identity without the fear that you would lose yourself. It is the development of intimacy that makes the retention of a mate possible. When this type of intimacy is in the process of developing during early adolescence, boyfriends and girlfriends often change. Unless the sense of personal identity and intimacy subsequently develops, the basis of a stable, long-term relationship with a mate is missing.

The adolescent also glimpses, for the first time, the sense that personal freedom is tied to insight into oneself. We almost never think of freedom as being connected with the inner quest for personal development. Freedom is usually associated with a socially liberal environment. Freedom in this sense involves the ability to be protected from unpredictable demands from other persons, organizations, or government.

But the quest for insight and personal freedom appears to engage almost everybody. It is a reflection of self-awareness that first comes to view in adolescence. It is the ability to overcome the restrictions and pressures of the world as we find them by substituting our own goals and purposes. We find our goals from understanding ourselves, and we achieve success by developing our resources as fully as they can be developed.

Gaining experience can be an exasperating challenge. Many experiences are closed to adolescents because of their age. An adolescent cannot own an automobile in many states, because minors cannot assume such responsibility. Liquor and beer are often forbidden. Certain movies are rated so that adolescents are supposed to be excluded. The laws and regulations for adolescents appear arbitrary to them. Thus breaking the law does not appear to be a major transgression to them. When adolescents break the law, usually it is viewed by them as a way of doing what seems rightfully theirs.

One way of coping with this paradox was the development of the liberal arts college. This college was originally a place where young people could broaden their experiences through discussion and thought, learn the basics of knowledge, and carry on high jinks under the protection of a permissive charter that colleges usually enjoy from local authorities. For example, beer has flowed profusely to freshmen in many colleges, even though the legal drinking age has been 21 or 18 years of age in most states. The liberal arts college has been a place where the official rules could be broken without making a public fuss. The uprisings on campuses of the past decade reflect efforts to push this independence much beyond its original intention.

The quest for experience and the willingness to live life to its extreme are the ways adolescents test themselves. Nobody has successfully explained the reasons for the awakening desire of some persons to pursue the experiences of life and probe their inner thoughts in a critical manner. Nor has anybody explained why certain people can look deeper into the recesses of their minds and withstand greater stress than others. Probably little can be done to change this pattern, and help for those adolescents who lose control of their lives often appears to reflect the helpfulness which surrounds therapy.

A great amount of experience is usually beneficial and liberating. It gives scope and reality to words that previously held little meaning. An adolescent needs the experience of seeing how the world actually works, learning which skills are needed for various occupations, judging how to act under various social situations, discovering which characteristics are enlivening and comforting to friends and a mate. Nobody knows, least of all the developing adolescent, which experiences eventually will be most meaningful.

The greatest waste is a talent that is never awakened. There have been literally hundreds of musicians with the talent of a Mozart who lived at a time when music was still undeveloped, lived in a village where music was unpracticed, or lived in a situation where the burden of making a living at an early age left no surplus of time or money to learn music. The same holds for engineering, chemistry, mathematics, and an almost unending list of skills. There are arts and sciences which are yet to be discovered, and large numbers of people could enrich themselves and their society if these arts and sciences were known to us now. That vision, of course, is beyond the power of each of us to fulfill. But we can begin, in a small way, with those about us who are adolescents and be sure that they learn what interests them. And those who are adolescents can explore their talents and identity to the fullest. That would be an accomplishment which would bear rewards for a lifetime.

Chapter 6

THE FINANCIAL STRATEGY OF ADOLESCENCE: KNOWLEDGE IS MONEY

*Y*OU need to know your talents before you can achieve anything of value. The idea that knowledge is money is the practical application of this philosophy. An adolescent inherently grasps this idea and sees its excitement. Adolescence is the first time when knowledge of yourself and the world around you is most important.

The financial strategies during adolescence involve an understanding that principles, not expediency, should be the guide to conducting one's finances. Of course, each person must meet many daily financial problems and solve them as best as possible without broad financial principles. But an adolescent sees the importance of trying, wherever possible, to guide his or her life according to the right principles, even though the benefits may involve long-term development and not show immediate benefits.

There are five financial strategies for the period of adolescence: (1) get an education, (2) be prepared to borrow to finance your education, (3) develop a savings habit, (4) build a good credit record, and (5) gain work experience.

KEY FINANCIAL GOALS OF ADOLESCENCE

Education is Important

This is the time for training and the development of your skills. You need to demonstrate to yourself and to others that you can acquire key skills that you may use throughout the remainder of your life cycle.

You should plan to put yourself in a variety of learning experiences, so that you can understand which types of skills you enjoy and can handle with ease. The value of education is that it can compress learning experience into a shorter period than if you were to apprentice a skilled person. Moreover, in many types of skills, it is no longer possible to be an apprentice to a skilled person. Many skilled professions and trades, from surgeons to electricians, require a prescribed period of education.

The emphasis on education and development of skills should not mean that you should lose your sense of perspective about the important social aspects of this period. Rather, you should try to integrate your social and educational activities. If you attend a high school or a college, your educational and social activities coexist, and you would likely be aware of both activities.

The problem of lack of education more often occurs among adolescents who complete high school, enter the work force, and discontinue efforts to continue to upgrade their skills. These persons usually do not invest enough in themselves during this stage of the life cycle. They often let the years pass them by without taking the extra effort to pursue an interest as far as possible. Then, for the remainder of their lives, they may find that they lack the technical background that would be needed to enable them to achieve their fullest potential in their work.

Be Prepared to Borrow to Finance Your Education

You should not let a lack of money deter you from obtaining the training you need. Whatever interest you choose to follow, you need to obtain training to practice that skill. This education is too important to let a lack of money keep you from your interest. Scholarships may be available, but if you do not obtain one, you should not be discouraged. You should borrow.

Some adolescents have a strong aversion to borrowing. These adolescents may have seen the costs of large consumer borrowing by their parents, and they may wish to avoid that pressure and concern. Others may have been raised in a conservative tradition that avoids borrowing from a moral point of view. Still others may instinctively avoid borrowing, because they do not feel comfortable being in a debtor's position.

There is nothing dishonorable about a loan. You are borrowing money for a business purpose. Your loan is to make you more productive and more valuable as a worker, and you should earn a higher income as a result of your training. This purpose is no different from that of the borrowing of a company to equip itself better.

Develop a Savings Habit

You should use virtually all of your income for living expenses or for the development of your skills and education. In fact, it would be a mistake if you tried to save a large percentage of your income now. Most likely, this money would be better used in the development of your skills.

Nevertheless, you should accumulate a basic savings account to give you some flexibility in managing your money, and you should begin a pattern of savings. But accumulating a large amount of savings is not the objective of this stage of your life cycle. This is the time to acquire experience to give you perspectives about yourself and to understand the ways of the world.

The principle of savings is important. You should save for immediate needs, such as gifts or things that you need, and through this pattern, you will see the importance of an accumulation of money that is greater than your day-to-day needs. In later stages of your life cycle, you should increase your savings rate, but the principle of using money to accomplish a very personal goal will remain the same. Savings concentrates the power of money to accomplish your objectives. The principle, not the amount, is what is important in this period of the life cycle.

Build a Good Credit Record

You should take the steps that are necessary to prove that you can handle the responsibilities of credit and a loan. A good credit record will be critical to you during the next stage of your life cycle, when you will build your leverage. At that time you will need the reputation that you will be developing during this period.

Whatever credit you take, you will pay back. If you find yourself with payments that are larger than your ability to repay, you will work out new arrangements with your lenders, but you will not seek bankruptcy voluntarily. The stakes are too high in the future for you to blemish your record at this stage of your life cycle. In the future you may wish to leverage yourself to buy a business or to make a major investment. A record of always repaying your debts may then make the difference between your receiving or not receiving financing at that time.

Credit is a magnificent creation. It enables someone who has greater opportunities than money to develop those opportunities. It does have certain basic rules that must be followed. You need to understand these rules which are discussed later and comply with them. If you do, the opening of the door of credit can be the opening of the door of an opportunity to fulfill your hopes.

Gain Work Experience

You need to have an understanding of the way the commercial world operates. You can learn this only from work experience. This experience is needed as you consider your skills and how they fit into business. This may be accomplished while you are in school. Many secondary schools and community colleges grant credit toward graduation based on work experience.

In addition, work can provide you with the income to pay for the training of your skills. Training and education have become increasingly expensive in recent years, and you may want to finance your training with a combination of work and a loan.

The most important aspect of your work experience is its effect on how you see yourself. If you use work to try out your talents, you will fulfill the purpose of work during this stage of the life cycle. With the exception of situations in which the money is essential to sustain you or others who are close to you, income from work is second in importance to this discovery of your inherent gifts and talents.

You should keep in mind which work you enjoy, and which work you seem to be unable to perform with interest and accomplishment. Virtually every job, no matter how senior it may be, is composed of pieces of work that you can now perform. One president of a major corporation once told his staff that they did some of the same work that he did, only he did more of it. What he meant was that he understood the significance of the work of his staff better than they did. You need to develop the same objectivity toward your work. You need to use work as a mirror to see yourself.

Relative Importance of Income and Expenses in Each Stage of the Life Cycle

Life Cycle Stage	Income				Expenses										
	Wages/ Salary	Secondary Occupation/ Avocation	Wages/ Salary of Spouse	Invest- ment Income	Hous- ing	Food	Cloth- ing	Trans- porta- tion	Educa- tion	Enter- tain- ment	Life Insurance	Other Expenses	Gifts	Income Taxes	Profit (Savings)
Adolescence	3	3													
Adult	3	3			2		5	4	1	2	5			4	1
Midlife			4		4				2	5	5			1	
Maturity	3	3							1	2				2	1
Age and Simplicity				4									5		

KEY INCOME AND EXPENSE CATEGORIES

The accompanying chart shows the 15 key categories of each person's income and expenses in the adolescent stage as well as for the four subsequent stages of the life cycle. The relative importance of each category of income and expense for a particular stage of the life cycle is also indicated.

The table shows that education, entertainment, a secondary occupation, transportation, and clothing represent the most important categories during the adolescent stage. These categories are important because they have a major impact on the adolescent's life. Nevertheless, in certain cases the dollar amounts may not be large, and you should not consider the size of spending to be the only, or even the major consideration in assessing the importance of a part of your budget.

Subsequent chapters cover the income and spending patterns of the remaining four stages of the life cycle.

Education Is Important to You

The most important issue that you now face is how to obtain the proper training for your talents. You are now awakening to your talents, and this discovery carries an enormous emotional charge. Nevertheless, you believe that you are ready for a period of training, and you have a willingness to undertake the sacrifices that are necessary with any training.

You need two kinds of education to fulfill the work challenge of this stage of the life cycle: technical training and the development of a personable manner among workers or customers. Both are essential for you to be able to make your way in a commercial environment.

Technical skills include such widely known activities as drafting, computer programming, mechanical repairing, surgery, pleading in court, typing, cooking, and so forth. In learning these technical skills, there is no substitute for knowing exactly how a line should be drawn, a letter should be typed, an incision should be cut, or which words should be spoken before a judge and jury. People who are skilled at their trades build everything we use and keep these things in repair.

Nevertheless, we also live in a highly interdependent society. Virtually everything we do involves other people, and their reaction to our presence helps determine the quality of our work. For example, the work of congenial groups tends to excel in quality. The productive effort of these people is directed to their work, not misdirected by disagreements and misunderstandings. I have observed that customers sense this cooperative attitude and tend to buy from representatives of congenial groups.

Each trade and profession has its own culture. Acceptable behavior and language among one group often is not acceptable in another group. Many persons fail at their jobs because they lack an understanding of the culture in which they now participate. I believe that relatively few persons fail in their work because of a lack of a particular type of technical training. And yet, ironically, this cultural aspect of education is frequently overlooked by adolescents. In many cases adolescents, as well as their parents, believe that where you receive your training makes little difference. What is important, they believe, is getting a sound technical education. Nothing could be more misleading. It is true that there is no good substitute for becoming competent in a skill, but your ability to be rewarded for your skills requires a blending of skills with the culture in which you work.

Education of both skills and culture reflects the choice of education following high school. Prior to graduating from high school, most adolescents have little choice in the selection of their education. They usually attend schools according to the requirements of their locality or community, although a relatively few adolescents attend private or parochial schools.

Nevertheless, from age 18 to 22, which represents the years following high school, you make a key decision in the choice of your further education. The choices include prestigious universities, community colleges, trade schools, the military services, on-the-job training, trade apprentices, to name the major choices. It is possible to learn a skill with each of these educational methods, but the culture among these choices is widely different.

For example, the prestige universities teach technical skills as well as the culture and the manner of the elite. There is a vast difference in culture between an Ivy League college and a state university. There is, however, virtually no difference in the content of information taught. The important difference between prestigious universities and less well-known colleges is not the intelligence of the students, nor the attitude of students toward studies, but differences of culture. The students attending regional colleges largely continue the culture that they have grown up with. In the Midwest, where I grew up, most students in local colleges reflected a middle-class, Midwestern culture. There was a strong sense of community among students, and there was a feeling that studies were not to interfere with this sense of community. The prestigious universities conveyed the importance of being on top as the worthwhile goal of life, and studies were one way of attaining that goal. Being on top meant winning a Nobel prize, being second meant being best in a scholarly field. Third was being a doctor or achieving a high level government or corporate position. Beyond that, nothing else mattered much. Clothes, manners, and speech made students comfortable with these goals.

The income statistics show that if you graduate from college, you should earn significantly more than if you did not attend, and if you graduated from any Ivy League college, you should earn much more than if you attended another school. The figures suggest that if you want to earn a high income, you should become comfortable with the culture of the elite, and if you are not from an elite background, you should attend an elite college.

Yet this conclusion is not the way to plan a life. Most adolescents would be under great strain in an elite environment. You don't have to follow the statistical route for success in education or anything else. There are enormous opportunities in other directions. Most importantly, the ultimate purpose of work is not to earn income, but to develop yourself so that your strengths are fulfilled. Following the statistical course to maximize your income would put a mental straitjacket on most people. Even if they were successful, they would have to suppress such an emotional strain that their creative energies could easily be exhausted, and their real strengths might remain neglected throughout their lifetime.

For example, a college friend was one of the most carefully cultivated men on campus. He was from a middle-class background, and he joined the most socially prominent fraternity. He had become an arbiter of good taste. His grades were satisfactory, but he appeared to be bored with his studies. After graduation, he went to work for a specialist firm on the New York Stock Exchange, and within a few years he became a partner of that firm. He had done all the right things to become a highly respected, very highly paid member of the financial community. Nevertheless, when he entered the midlife stage of his life cycle, he abandoned this image of himself and bought a farm in Vermont. He now works the farm, and the last I heard, he was happier than he had ever been.

This person recognized his true interest only after he had lived almost two decades of his life to pursue a goal that had little meaning to him. Those years could have been spent developing his interest in agriculture. They probably would have been happier years, and he might have achieved prominence in agriculture which might now be unavailable to him. The mistake, I believe, was that in his adolescence he did not come to grips with the cost of pretending to be somebody that he was not. He allowed the surface glamor of success in a prestigious company to mislead him from himself.

There is another area of education beside the formal training in colleges and universities. Trades and skills of craftsmen, graphics skills, computer skills, and construction skills represent only a few of these. They are taught through unions, company training programs, community colleges, and private trade schools. Among that group, private trade schools are probably the most efficient educational schools in existence. They are dedicated to the teaching of fundamental skills quickly and economically. Trade schools are in business to enable their students to pass certifying examinations and practice their trade safely.

In recent years the compensation of tradesmen has risen sharply relative to most other economic groups. A friend who handles pensions for electricians in a major industrial city recently showed me data indicating that the average income from electricians was similar to that of senior vice presidents of local banks. Moreover, these union workers enjoyed more job security than their banker counterparts. There is no longer any financial inferiority to many trade and craft positions.

The remainder of the working population has little education in skills. These people are engaged in such occupations as waiters, messengers, assembly-line workers, and construction laborers, to name only a few. The jobs are usually among the lowest paid and offer relatively little job security. They usually offer little opportunity to develop one's talents. There are exceptions, of course. Most families include a grandmother who emigrated to this country, worked as a seamstress, and made heirloom pillows and comforters that have been handed down generations. The work was hard and long, but the effort occasionally produced an object of beauty. Nevertheless, most jobs that require little or no training involve repetitious actions and provide little personal development. The world is full of people who work, as Thoreau said, in quiet desperation.

The most important issue you face is to discover which activity gives you the most pleasure. Most adolescents have an inkling of the activities that give them the greatest personal satisfaction. Some follow their talents without a distraction. But most adolescents feel that the wishes or hopes of their parents or guardians may pull them in another direction. That conflict should be resolved promptly, since the only work that you can endure in good times as well as poor times is that which gives you personal enjoyment.

Whichever vocation is chosen, some type of education will probably be needed. Education almost always involves a cost. In some instances, such as medical or scientific education, the cost is large. Currently, it requires the payment of more than $100,000 in fees and living costs to educate a medical doctor, and that cost will probably continue to rise. It costs almost as much to educate a college professor or a space physicist.

These large sums may be a deterrent to low-income families as well as many middle-income families. Most adolescents who approach such an educational expense cannot pay the cost unless they receive scholarships, financial support from their parents, and some form of employment. Nevertheless, most educational expenses involve more moderate amounts. Many instances, such as apprenticeship periods for trades, involve no direct expense. The apprenticeship trainees receive an income as they learn their skill.

A dedication to the importance of this personal investment is essential. The dedication almost always reflects a strong desire to learn a skill as part of personal fulfillment. Without a strong sense of this need, any educational program cannot be sustained. Whenever I talk with students who have dropped out of college, the message they convey to me is that the essential element of achieving personal fulfillment through their education was missing.

Work

The purpose of work for an adolescent is not to earn a lot of money. Rather, in this period you should gain experience in learning how to link your skills with your earning power. In this period, you should use work to learn the commercial way of conducting yourself. Work is an alternative to education for adolescents. At times, it may be a better alternative. It almost always is a useful supplement to education.

Most often an adolescent is hired for abilities and training which he or she already possesses. Sometimes an employer will provide a minimal amount of training. Almost always this training involves procedures in the operations of a business, and the knowledge which is learned is immediately used. Often, new skills are put to use within an hour.

The great advantage of this type of learning experience is its close link between skills and earnings. Many adolescents come from homes where there is no clear connection between knowledge and the value of that knowledge. Many adolescents grow up in families where they do not handle money and have little appreciation of the way people exchange their skills for money. A job can be a very broadening experience for these adolescents.

One of my high school friends was from a family of very modest means, and this friend wanted to become a medical doctor. He developed this interest, he later told me, as he worked as a check-out boy in a local supermarket. He had always been a good student, but before this job, he had never given much thought to a career. As he loaded groceries into bags and carried the bags to cars, he discovered that this type of work was dull for him. Yet he liked cars, and whenever he placed groceries in the trunk of cars he liked, he would talk to the owners. He found that the owners of many of the cars he liked were doctors' wives. He then realized that carrying out groceries would not provide him with enough money to pay his way through medical school, much less college. So he began to study automobile repairs. He went to the public library, borrowed several books which showed how basic repairs are made, and got a part-time job as an auto mechanic at four times the hourly rate that he received as grocery boy. His work with auto mechanics proved to be an eye-opener. He had never used his hands in a skilled way before, and he enjoyed the work immensely, particularly mechanical work requiring a sense of feel or touch. In those days, there was no electronic equipment, and tune-ups were largely a matter of manual adjustments using a feeler guage to make a car run smoother. He became known locally as the best person to tune-up cars. His income from auto mechanics largely paid for his undergraduate education. He borrowed money and received a scholarship to medical school, and he is now one of the nation's leading eye surgeons.

Another friend also used his work as a key part of his education, but in a different manner. This friend always thought of himself as a financier and dreamed of being manager of a major stock brokerage firm. His first job selling stock proved to be a failure, as did his second job selling bonds. He had completed his college education in the mean-time, so these two job failures came as a major blow. After he left his second job, he took an odd job in a department store and did volunteer work for the Boy Scouts.

Within six months his work with the Boy Scouts was regarded so highly that the organization asked him to join them. His ability to make scouting fun and meaningful was exactly what the organization needed. He enjoyed the work, but the pay was low, and he felt that he could not make a career from scouting.

He then decided to return to a university to study for an educational administration degree. His wife worked to support him during these years. Although he was not an outstanding student, he worked diligently and received a doctorate in education. Today, he is president of a small private college in the Midwest. He sits in an office that is more luxurious than most presidents of brokerage firms, and he has honor and respect that certainly exceed that of broker-age officials. He also has many occasions to give speeches, which he always was fond of making. He is happier than almost anybody I know.

The experience of finding a job and being called upon to perform work is one of the key ways that you discover your talents. The biggest stumbling block to getting a job is getting started. Adolescents are almost always embarrassed as soon as they take the first step to approach a prospective employer. There is nothing embarrassing about asking for a job. Yet it always appears so the first time. Once you have passed the hurdle of asking for a job, the most difficult part of finding a job is over.

The preparation of a simple resume is an essential step in seeking your first job. If your school offers a course or training in this area, be sure to sign up. You should prepare a resume and hand it to your prospective employer at the beginning of the job interview. Most adolescents think that the preparation of a resume is too much work, and they seldom prepare one. This is a mistake. Your first resume will take no more than two hours to complete, and after you have prepared it, you will feel self-confident when you approach your prospective boss. You will wonder how anybody would want to get a job without one. A resume gives you a chance to look at yourself with candor and pride. That is a big step toward the confidence you need when you look for work.

Your resume should show your name, address, and telephone number in the upper-left corner. Next, in the main part of the paper, it should show where you went to school, listing addresses and telephone numbers. You might mention your grade average if it is good. Always mention your best grades and subjects. After a space, you should describe, in one or two sentences, several of you best achievements. The accomplishments don't have to be school related, but they should show initiative. Perhaps you alerted someone's mother of a child that was in danger, or you cleaned up a camp cabin when nobody would do it. Include any other jobs that involved responsibility, such as baby sitting, caring for pets or household plants for vacationing owners, or teaching Sunday school classes. These are types of achievements that convey a sense of responsibility and initiative to an employer, and employers like those personality characteristics. Leave another space, and list some of your hobbies or sports. Finally, give the name, address, and telephone number of two persons who you believe will give a good recommendation for you. You should approach these people for their help before you use their names. You may also wish to include your date of birth. That's it. You now have your first resume.

Sample Resume for an Adolescent

June R. Harper
2125 Wren Avenue
Waters Glen, Ohio 44132
(216) 743-2746

Education

> Waters Glen High School
> 535 River Street
> Waters Glen, Ohio 44132
> Graduated, June 1981
>
>> Counsellor—Mrs. Mary Wertheim—625-4140
>>
>> Maintained a B average for three years
>>
>> Courses included English, Mathematics, Home Economics and Woodshop

Achievements

> Organized the school "Walkathon" for disabled children, which raised enough money to send a disabled child to summer camp—spring 1981
>
> Girls' varsity basketball team—Forward—Team won second place in north county tournament— 1980 to 1981 season
>
> Won second place in Rotary Club public speaking contest—autumn 1980

References

> Mr. John Troutman, owner, Troutman Music Center, 245 Center Street, Waters Glen, Ohio 44132. Phone 624-6574
>
> Mary Jensen, M.D., 658 Stanton Street, Waters Glen, Ohio 44132. Phone 624-5438
>
> Date of birth—October 16, 1963

You should type the resume, or ask someone who can type to do this for you. Then take your resume to a copy center and get it copied. You will give prospective employers a copy, and you should keep the original. When you hand your resume to your prospective employer, this person will be favorably impressed, because most adolescents don't do this. Most importantly, you will feel confidence you never expected to feel, which at that moment will be just what you need.

Perhaps the most important change that has occurred in the past generation in the work force has been the new role of women. Today, most women believe that they will work during some part, if not all of the years between their twenties and sixties. When I started work, in the 1950s, relatively few women expected to spend much time, if any at all, in the work force. Moreover, along with the greater participation, women have begun to demand higher recognition for their work contribution.

Thus today there are important differences in the way women perceive their place in the work force. The younger women often see themselves as equals to men, while the older women are usually more reticent about asserting their position in business. This book tries to reflect this important difference of perception of women in the work force, and it offers suggestions that would apply to the mainstream of women in each stage of the life cycle. Because of differences in perception, the comments will differ as the life cycle progresses. Thus, for example, it requires little encouragement for an adolescent girl to look for a job, but many women who are in their maturity or midlife stage of the life cycle may require considerable support and assistance as they take that step.

Entertainment

In this stage of your life cycle, you should give special attention to entertainment. Meeting a wide range of people, comparing experiences, and dating are essential activities of this stage. The costs of entertainment usually have little effect on the value of the entertainment. Entertainment adds to your understanding of yourself, your interests, and your friends. It is as available at a high school dance as it is on a skiing weekend. Cost isn't crucial.

Strange as it may sound, the major problem of entertainment spending of adolescents is not overspending, but underspending. Overspending usually reflects overindulgence, and that occasion can provide a valuable lesson about controlling personal spending. When it occurs, the amount of overspending is usually not so much that it will cripple a budget for a long period. Overspending on entertainment may be the best place to learn about the limits of a budget. Rather, if underspending reflects a fear of meeting other people and associating with groups, it can reflect a major problem. Some adolescents hoard their money to compensate for their lack of association with others. Saving money can become a substitute for developing friendships. Sometimes the spending of money for entertainment may get this person into circulation with other people. In this situation, spending money for entertainment may be an important step in an adolescent's development.

Transportation

The key to freedom, in the eyes of adolescents, is an automobile. A car is the vehicle of escape from what adolescents believe to be a stuffy, dull adult world. It brings adolescents to each other.

No wonder the automobile is a major interest, and often a major expense to adolescents. There is no other means of transportation that is quite so perfect. It is immediately available, it is quicker than most other transportation, and it is private.

Cars are expensive, and they are often a major budget expense to adolescents who purchase them. Ironically, the purchase of a car is usually an adolescent's first introduction into the commercial world. The purchase of a car requires an accumulation of money, either for full payment or for a down payment. If a car is bought on time, a down payment, the responsibilities for borrowing, and insurance present a new experience of personal finance. They represent a snapshot of the commercial world.

The way an adolescent handles automobile finances, including operating expenses, often sets a pattern of how he or she handles other expenses in the future. I have noticed that adolescents who finance their first car, with their parents as cosigners, are often major users of personal credit in later stages of their life cycle. In contrast, one friend bought his first car with cash and prides himself that he never borrowed to buy a car. He is now retired, and says he has owned sixteen cars.

Probably nothing seasons an adolescent to the ways of the commercial world faster than a car that breaks down. It is always an emotional experience. Nevertheless, if you think through the problem carefully, you will have made a big step in your financial development. If your decision is to sell a car that is not working right, at a loss, you will never be the same as before. You will look at cars, and everything else, with a more critical eye.

There is a role for public transportation, which includes buses, trains and other people's cars. Buses and trains certainly are not glamorous, but are much less expensive than owning a car. The most overlooked form of public transportation is someone else's car. If you want to develop this type of transportation, you should always offer a few dollars for gas to the driver. It's the cheapest and best transportation available. If you help pay for the cost of transportation, you will be sought as a rider.

KEY ASSETS AND LIABILITIES

The accompanying table shows fourteen key categories of a balance sheet for an adolescent for five stages of the life cycle. As was noted with the table for the income statement, the relative importance of the categories is indicated, and subsequent chapters refer to this table.

Relative Importance of Assets and Liabilities
in Each Stage of the Life Cycle

Life Cycle Stage	Assets (Uses of Funds)									Liabilities (Source of Funds)				
	Checking Account	Savings Account	Home	Real Estate	Life Insurance	Mineral Invest-ments	Debt Financial Invest-ments	Equity Financial Invest-ments	Antique Invest-ments	Bank Loan	Personal Loan Co.	Credit Union	Family	Friends
Adolescence	2	3								1			4	
Adult		3	1	4	2					3		5		
Midlife				3	5	4	1	1		2		5	4	5
Maturity				4		3	2	2						
Age and Simplicity							1		5					

Bank Loan

One of the most important business associations you will make during adolescence is a bank lending officer. A loan for a car, furniture, or a boat is often the step that brings you to meet this person. Many other types of financial institutions provide loans, but they either require you to pledge your savings account with them (which means you must first have savings), or they are permitted to make loans only for specific purposes. For example, savings and loan associations are permitted to make loans for homes and real estate purposes, but they are not permitted to make loans for automobiles. If you don't have a savings account to borrow against, you have to borrow elsewhere.

In most cases, banks are also the lowest-cost lender. Some specialty lenders, such as credit unions, may offer loans for particular purposes at lower rates. But for most consumer loans, bank rates for borrowing are lower than the rates of other lenders. Most other financial institutions obtain part of their funds from banks and mark up the rate of interest that they charge accordingly.

Often adolescents arrange their borrowing from the merchant who sells a product. They may feel intimidated by a bank. You should not be bothered by these impressions, since they reflect a lack of experience. Rather, you should shop for the lowest interest rates. Your shopping list should include at least one bank, since the cornerstone of your borrowing should be a bank loan officer. In the long run, this person can help you with money more than any other financial person.

After you receive a loan, you will always make payments on the date the payments are due. This is the most important advice you will ever receive concerning credit. Your record of meeting your commitments, always on time, gives you more bonus points with lenders than anything else you can do. In fact, without a record of prompt payment, you will have a poor credit rating, no matter how high your income may rise. Lenders want only one thing from you when you borrow. They want their money back when they expect it to be returned. The whole story of borrowing is that simple.

There may be times when you find that it will be difficult or impossible to make payments on schedule. You may have a sudden expense because of a death in your family, or Christmas expenses may get out of hand, or your vacation trip may end up with a splurge. These things happen to everybody. First, you should try to make your payment by cutting back on other expenses. You may eat beans and sandwiches for a few days and watch television for a few Saturday nights. If these cutbacks are not enough, you should speak with your lender and tell that person that you cannot make the full payment, but that you can make a token payment. The lender will make a note on your payment record that you were not delinquent, and your credit record will not be downgraded. Of course, you don't want to make such a request very frequently.

You may take on more debt than you can handle. This often happens when you get a job, move out of your parents' home, and underestimate how expensive current costs really are. In a flurry, you also may buy too many clothes or buy an expensive stereo or a car. A few months later, you may find yourself with delinquent payments. Other times on your job you may encounter several slow months, but payments on debts keep coming due regardless of lower income. These situations may require new loans to consolidate other loans and reduce the dollar amount of monthly payments by extending the number of payments. They may require the sale of some of the purchases as well, to lighten the overall debt burden.

Whatever the solution, you should approach your lending officer before the problem becomes acute and ask for advice. This is not a pleasant moment, and it may be embarrassing to you. But don't worry about your embarrassment. And don't become angry at your lenders. Your main concern should be your credit record. If you reach a solution before you accumulate many delinquency notices, you should not damage that record.

Checking Account

The next important step in your financial management as an adolescent is to open a checking account. Many adolescents believe that a checking account is a luxury and that they can take care of their financial transactions by cash. When they need to send money by mail, they purchase a money order. This is a mistake. You should open a checking account at this time to establish yourself as a reliable person in handling your money. A checking account provides a clear record of this ability, and it is this record which is important to you.

A checking account shows a bank that you can budget successfully. Even if you write only a few checks a month, the ability to keep your checking account in balance shows that you are careful and accurate in the way you manage your money.

After you have established a checking account, and possibly borrowed money, you will have taken key steps in building a credit record. If you need additional loans, you should return to your principal lender. You should avoid going to various merchants and borrowing from them, one on top of the other. Compounding your lenders is a sure way to lose control over your budget, and this type of borrowing is an expensive way to finance yourself. Your checking account can provide a central control over your budget. If you use it in this manner, you should have a clear idea of where your finances stand at all times.

Savings Account

The purpose of a savings account is convenience and safety and a place to keep money you have earmarked to buy a car, for Christmas presents, for a vacation, to pay for next term's tuition, or other purposes that require a moderate amount of money. For many adolescents a savings account may be a place to put money for no specific purpose but for the longer-term purpose of having money available when it would be needed. It is a bit inconvenient to withdraw savings, more so than cashing a check. Yet it is not so inconvenient that taking money out of a savings account represents a hardship. Some adolescents like the buffer of a savings account. It makes them think twice before they spend money, and keeps their impulse buying to manageable amounts.

You should open a passbook savings account. The longer-term certificates pay a higher rate of interest, but high interest rates are not your first consideration. NOW accounts give you more liquidity, but their net yield sometimes is lower than savings accounts, and for your purposes, the added small liquidity of NOW accounts is not critical. You should have flexibility in the use of your money. You want to be able to follow your interests, and as your interests change, you should have your money available to follow those changes. You should not now be concerned with making long-term investments, whether in certificates of deposit or real estate.

You should be sure that your savings account is growing fast enough for your needs. If you are saving to buy a car, you should determine what the cost or down payment of the car will amount to. You may need to determine how much you can cut back your consumption and living expenses. You may consider finding a job or changing your job to one that pays more. All these considerations have an impact on your savings account, and this account represents a key barometer of many other personal and financial decisions that you make.

Family

Another source of financing for an adolescent is the family. Historically, families have been the traditional source of financing for an adolescent. Before there were banks, insurance companies, and the large financial institutions of today, families were the basic financial entities. In fact, the emergence of banking during the late middle ages was really the development of wealthy families who went into the business of lending money. In areas of the world where banking presently is limited, such as in the tribal areas of Africa or in Communist countries, wealth continues to be accumulated on a private basis and distributed to other persons largely through families.

The family still represents an important financial resource to an adolescent, but the family should be regarded as only a temporary source of funds. You should develop a reputation for the careful handling of money among commercial lenders, and this can be achieved only if you develop a direct relationship with banks, savings and loan associations, and other financial companies. A good credit reputation among public lenders involves your building a record of performance. A family is a private arrangement in which there is no public record, and often payback requirements are softened out of personal considerations. You will achieve the credit reputation that you need in later stages of your life cycle only when you are able to stand on your own before public financial institutions.

The financing of education represents one of the major shifts in the way our society views the relationship between parents and adolescents. Today, fewer parents believe that they have an obligation to give their children the best education possible. Many parents now think of themselves first and their adolescents' education second. You may find that your parents do not stress the importance of education and may not give you the incentive to obtain the best education for your needs because they do not want to spend the money. Most parents will not say this explicitly, and few would even wish to look at their spending in this light. There is nothing wrong with this point of view. Don't fight your parents on this issue. If you disagree, accept their thinking. The incentive for getting the best skills is your responsibility, not theirs.

In this case, you should ask your parents for a loan. Obtain a standard form for a personal note from a stationery store and present the note to your parents with your signature. If you are borrowing for an education, charge yourself a minimal rate of interest. If the purpose of your loan is to buy a car, stereo, or other personal possession, you should charge yourself the going rate for personal loans at banks. You should also clearly indicate your intention to make regular payments according to the terms of the loan. Few parents would turn down such a request, if they have the money.

At age 35, it will make little difference whether you borrowed from your parents or they gave you the money for an education, a car, or whatever you need. But if you live up to your agreement to repay the amount regularly, you will have made a giant step forward. The habit of living up to a promise is more valuable than owning all of the gold in the world. That confidence would be of great value to you in a later state of your life, when you need to be prepared to accept major long-term obligations.

Chapter 7

ADULTHOOD AND THE NEST EGG: AGE 23 TO 35

*T*HE adulthood stage of the life cycle is a period when you are in the saddle, so far as you see your life. This is an age of strength, of full awareness of your talents and, more importantly, the power of those talents. It is a time of working and building, with an overall sense of satisfaction with what you are accomplishing.

Adulthood is a time when you feel on top of the world. You have greater physical stamina than at any other age of your life cycle. You can make mistakes and bounce back, and you sense the considerable advantage of this inherent recuperative power. You often feel a bit impatient with people who are slower, less fit, or less capable than you.

The question adulthood asks is how to live with energy and strength. Nevertheless, there are important boundaries to your strength which you accept. These boundaries include working in a somewhat subordinate position as you learn your trade. Most persons in the adulthood stage accept the boundaries to their activities, because they believe that they will inevitably move beyond them, and pushing too hard isn't necessary. Time is on the side of persons in this stage of the life cycle.

Living with strength gives a feeling of surplus during this stage of the life cycle. It can be a wonderful feeling and give a sense of well-being that is not enjoyed at any other period of life. It reflects the feeling that there is ample energy, abundance, and humanity for all to share. These persons have a growing confidence in their abilities, which gives them a willingness to accomplish difficult, prolonged projects. Many persons in adulthood seek particularly difficult challenges, in order to immerse themselves into activities that demonstrate their powers.

Underlying all these activities is a faith in your ability to progress and develop. You believe that you will become a more talented and valuable person in the future. This underlying faith sustains you through difficulties. You see reversals as being temporary, and you bounce back with renewed strength, because you can see the benefits you hope to achieve in your mind's eye.

The weakness of this stage of the life cycle occurs if you jump too far or too fast, to miss the training that work requires. If you miss the details, the fine points, the finesse that the mastery of any skill requires, you will miss the best, and perhaps the only real opportunity to know a subject as well as is humanly possible. Never again will you have both the energy and the feeling that you have the time to learn something well, or delve deeply into a way of life that you believe in. If you overlook the need to develop your skills during this period, you will probably find yourself technically weak for the remainder of your life. The shortcomings of not developing your skills during this stage of the life cycle can be overcome later, but only with much effort, and often with considerable sacrifice.

During the adulthood period, there are two key purposes of life—work and loved ones. Of these two purposes, the most important is probably finding the way to build deep, lasting human relationships. The preceding period of adolescence was one of frequent fights, even among friends. The adult-hood stage is calmer, with relatively few disagreements. You learn how to overlook unimportant matters, and your sense of self-confidence lets you keep your balance in controversies.

The value of this attitude is that it gives you toleration, which I believe is the basis of all lasting friendships. Each of us is different, and if we always focused on those differences, we would like nobody, and nothing ever would be accomplished. We learn how to be tolerant during the adulthood phase of our life cycle, and with it, we lay the basis of all of our long-term personal, social, and business relationships.

Perhaps the ultimate test of toleration is to live with one's spouse. I have always enjoyed stories about how spouses responded to this or that happening. These stories usually involve a friend's narration of some unpleasant or difficult situation and the spouse's tart reply, but willing acceptance of the situation. The stories, of course, have two points. They also show toleration between two people at its most critical point. Married people live closer together and have more opportunity to see imperfections than anybody else. If ever a person's toleration is fully tested, it is in marriage. I have never known anybody who was intimate with the same person for a long period who did not possess a large measure of toleration.

To fail at intimacy or toleration in marriage may forfeit, in some degree, mastery of subsequent stages of the life cycle. I have often met people who give every indication of being outstanding businessmen or businesswomen but failed to be tolerant after I knew them for a while. They were often in their thirties or were older. Many had been briefly married, had been divorced for several years, or had been married several times. In many instances I found their brilliance or special talents were marred by an undercurrent of intolerance about some key person, a major policy of the company, or something which made working with them difficult. Over a period of time it was as if they would build a barrier to me or to anybody who might become a close friend.

In practicing your skills, tolerance is essential if you are to achieve any long-lasting competence and acceptance by your associates. The tolerance one shows with friends carries over to managing a career, as well as managing money. Imperfections are ever with us, and mistakes will always be made. The ability to live with these less-than-perfect situations gives us the freedom to look to others and care about their welfare in a constructive manner. We then multiply our strength, as others carry our skills forward by their willingness to accept us and our skills.

The president of a major corporation I once worked for was suddenly confronted with a disaster in a key division. I was in the president's office discussing another subject when he answered the phone and learned of the situation. A large storage tank had exploded, many persons were injured, profits from the division would disappear for at least one quarter, and the legal liability of the corporation probably would be tested in court. The president's tone was serious as he learned of the magnitude of the damage, but he never blamed the manager of the division for the loss. He asked about plans for repairs, and he even joked at a small comment before he hung up. The conversation was exactly as I would have expected from a person who was tolerant in a difficult situation. His concern for the manager of the division was his primary interest at the time, and that required confidence in his position and tolerance.

Some people substitute close personal ties with another person with the company or institution for which they work. The success of many religious organizations in finding members over many centuries indicates that some people seek alternatives to close intimate ties with another person. Some modern-day executives in corporations are following this ancient pattern and have allowed the corporation to become a substitute for their wives or family. In addition, the armed forces, teaching, and certain professions include many people who have devoted their personal attention to the service of these institutions.

Toleration is important to your career. In fact, toleration is as essential with those who teach you skills as it is with close friends and loved ones. I have frequently observed that persons in their adult stage of the life cycle who have a family appear best able to grasp the problems of building a career, learning a skill, or developing their management skills. It is as if these people are confident enough of themselves to accept the differences of others without becoming defensive or upset. They tend to attract the best that other people offer, and they are able to try out these talents without fear of losing their own identity.

In developing a skill, perhaps the most important step is finding a mentor. This person is a master at his or her trade, business, or profession and is one with whom you are completely comfortable. In reading the biographies of many persons who have achieved considerable distinction in their work, I have been struck by the repeated credit these people give to a mentor. In business this person may be an established hand who takes special interest in a trainee during his or her initial years of work. In a profession, the person may be a senior judge or a talented surgeon who brings a young lawyer or doctor into his chambers or operating room to help and observe. In farming, trades, and all types of work, a mentor serves the same purpose.

For a person in the adulthood stage of life, to respond to a mentor requires patience. It is not always easy for a person who has the full powers of an adult to be willing to learn about his or her lack of skill. I have never observed a successful way that this paradox of strength and weakness has been bridged, except through a mentor. It is as if the mentor gives a sense of confidence that a skill can be learned, and that the shortcomings of the learner will prove to be temporary. There is a mutual tolerance when this transfer occurs. The mentor is tolerant of himself or herself, accepting those mistakes, but not forgetting them.

Persons who do not find mentors or do not accept them never seem to achieve their full potential in subsequent stages of their life cycle. One friend in college was particularly critical of all of his professors. He would invariably stress the weak points of these teachers and seldom would give credit to their strength. Several times he thought that he had found a professor who was perfect or someone in whom he had confidence, but the period was short-lived. This friend had considerable talent in English, which is a subject that requires imagination as well as hard work. He had the talents to fulfill both of these requirements. Yet, it is as if he has been stunted. From time to time I have kept in touch with him. His work is almost the same as I remember it was in college, but there has not been a progression or a development. I believe that his lack of accepting a mentor has been his major drawback in his career as an author and critic, and it has also held back his career as a teacher. His basic intolerance of others has been mainly responsible for his not finding a mentor.

Another friend is an auto mechanic. I have always wanted my car to run smoothly, and I keep a sharp eye for persons who have the talent to make cars run without vibration. A good auto mechanic requires a feel or touch to make any car run right, I believe, because the internal tolerances of all cars are quite different. The condition of metal, circuits, and stress of wear differs among engines, and when I find a good mechanic, I appreciate his talent.

One of the best mechanics I have come across was able to correct whatever problem my car had. He always made my car run the way I wanted. After he had been repairing my car for a year, I asked him how it was possible that he was able to take care of my car so much better than most other mechanics. The others had what appeared to me to be the same equipment, the same techniques, and the same instructions about repairing a car, and I wondered why they had not been as skillful. He said that he owed his ability to his first boss in Michigan. He had worked for General Motors as a young man, and since it was during the depression years of the 1930s, he felt grateful for the job. He had worked for over a year in an assembly job and did his job exactly as required. He was then transferred to an engine adjustment department and found that he was in a position that he felt was over his head. He followed the company's instructions exactly, but the cars he worked on were frequently rejected by the final inspectors. As he became more concerned, his boss took a particular interest in helping him and showed him how to use his judgment to work with the technical equipment. In those days, there was relatively little technical equipment, and he learned to rely on the feel of an engine as much as what the gauges showed him. He said that he had always been a person who never did things differently than instructions until that work experience, and that whatever talent he now possessed was due to the help his boss gave him years earlier.

I have observed that mentors provide much more than technical skill, as the mechanic alluded. They show style, demonstrate modes of conduct, and show how to approach problems in an acceptable manner. They express the way the social system works. All of us live in a social environment, and our work performance is evaluated in a large part by how well our work fits into the socially acceptable way of doing things. There are as many different social systems as there are organizations, and each has its peculiarities and rewards. Mentors understand these special aspects of a working environment and know how to pass along their insights.

The son of one friend was offered work as a manager of a warehouse in a large city. Since the salary was considerably higher than he could have obtained in his small home town, he gladly accepted the job. He told me that he did not look deeper into the background of the company because he reasoned that a warehouse manager could not get into trouble if he simply followed commonly accepted business practices. Unfortunately for this person, commonly accepted business practices with this company involved falsifying the records. This person was reluctant to accept that business practice, but he went along with it for several months. His wife, however, became increasingly nervous and urged him to leave. After seven months, he was offered another job with additional responsibility within the organization, which meant more responsibility for the falsified records. His wife made a decision for him to leave the company by packing their possessions and announced that they were moving immediately to some other location. One year later, after he had found other work, the company he had originally worked for filed for bankruptcy, and its officers were under investigation.

This incident points out the strengths and the weakness of the way you typically approach your work in this period. You often are a bit like a grammar school student toward your work. You are good at tasks, anxious for promotion, willing to accept the system in which you participate, and thus careful to follow the rules. You are perhaps more anxious to succeed in the eyes of your superiors than you are to weigh each task in its broad moral overtones. You tend to be more trusting than critical in your work and your superiors. You need to be sure that you can look upon your work with pride and be sure that it lives up to your long-term expectations.

The adulthood stage of the life cycle is a period of relatively little tension. The days of rides in fast cars, late-night rap sessions at the dorm, and heroic vistas of new learning are over. This narrowing in scope will not last for the remainder of your life, as another period will pick up the challenge that you now lay to rest. The narrowing of your scope has a purpose. It concentrates your energy and enables you to learn from others in ways that you need to understand.

You should enjoy yourself as you immerse yourself with your family, your work, and your culture. In this period, you choose ways to express yourself, your most personal associations, your way of working with things or ideas, and your values and philosophy.

This is a period of fitting into the way of life you wish to devote years of hard work. You want to be sure that your efforts will reflect a way of life that you can have pride in, because you are developing your basic skills. In subsequent periods of your life cycle, you will point to this period as the time that you built your base. Never again will you be able to work so many hours, or carry so large a burden on your shoulders. This is a time of quiet achievement.

Chapter 8

THE FINANCIAL STRATEGY OF ADULTHOOD: SAVINGS NEED TO BE STEADY

*T*HIS stage of your life cycle is the first time in your life that you are given full responsibility for your financial well-being. During most of your adolescent stage of the life cycle you had your parents, relatives, and friends to turn to if you found yourself in a financial scrape. Now, however, you are completely at the helm of your financial ship.

There are five key financial strategies for the adulthood period of the life cycle: (1) savings should be emphasized, (2) leverage is important, (3) both parties of a household should work, (4) you should develop an entrepreneurial skill, and (5) you should make friends who can help you develop your skills. These strategies involve the way you use your money as well as the way that you use your time. They are designed to enable you to build a financial base during this period, as well as a solid work experience.

You will want to use this financial base when you enter your next stage of the life cycle. You will then also appreciate the experience you will have developed in your work. Yet, during the adulthood stage, the steady, regular emphasis on building your base of financial and work experience may seem routine, possibly boring. There is nothing wrong with this direction. You are building your knowledge, reputation, and assets, and you should not worry about appearing to be dull.

KEY FINANCIAL GOALS OF ADULTHOOD

Savings Should Be Emphasized

Your financial profile shows one major weakness. You own virtually no net assets. The only exception to this situation is the small number of people who have inherited wealth. Your first financial goal is to build up your net worth, because net worth provides you with more flexibility in making plans than any other financial step you can take. Your net worth is your capital base, which is the heart of your financial profile. All other assets are built on this base.

There is no universal savings rate that is perfect for everybody. Nevertheless, as was noted earlier, a good savings target is 20 percent of your income. If your savings rate is appreciably below that rate, you should look carefully at the way you handle your money. You may not be saving enough. However, if your savings rate is considerably higher, you may have cut back your personal consumption to such low levels that you are living too frugally.

Most people in the adult stage perceive themselves as saving very little, or even saving nothing from month to month. If you look only at your net additions to your savings account, this may be true. (A net addition is the change in your account after all deposits and withdrawals have been made.) Your total savings is broader than net additions to your savings account. The accompanying table shows ten categories of savings, and you should include all of these categories in calculating your savings rate.

Calculation of Your Personal Savings Rate

Net additions to your checking account $_____

Net additions to your savings account _____

Payments on your home mortgage which reduce
    your mortgage _____

Payments on your automobile or other durable
    goods which reduce your remaining debt _____

Purchase of stock _____

Equity payments on real estate other than
    your home _____

Trust investments _____

Additions to the equity of insurance
    policies _____

Purchase of gold, silver, and precious
    gems _____

Other investments _____

    Total savings $_____

    Total income _____

    Savings rate (your savings
        divided by your income) _____%

How to Calculate Leverage

Purchase price of asset $_____

Equity cash you have put into the asset $_____

Multiple (or leverage) of purchase price
    of asset to your equity—divide
    purchase price by equity cash $_____

How to Calculate the Cash Flow of
Leveraged Asset

Income from asset $_____

Add: Special benefits (such as
        investment tax credit)   _____

Add: Tax value of depreciation   _____

Less: Cost of borrowing   _____

Less: Upkeep and maintenance expenses   _____

       Cash Flow   _____

Leverage Is Important

The accompanying table shows you how to calculate your leverage on an asset. It shows that leverage is simply the ratio of the purchase price of an asset to the equity you have put into it. Your leverage is a rough measure of your burden of risk. The higher the leverage, the greater is your risk.

The adulthood stage of your life cycle is the period when time is more completely on your side than in any other period. You have the longest life expectancy during this period, so you can handle long-term debt better than at any other period. A friend once mused that the one thing out of kilter with the world was that you are cash poor when you are young and cash rich when you are old. He meant that if you had a large amount of savings in your adulthood stage, you could leverage that amount and take financial control over assets that were considerably larger. You would then have many future years to reap the benefits of this leverage.

Most persons in their adulthood stage have relatively few assets they can use for leverage. Some persons have no assets. You should begin somewhere, and even if your leverage potential is limited, you should use some part of it.

There are limits to the leverage multiple that you should carry, and it is important to keep these limits in mind. It would be foolhardy to take on risks or obligations that lie beyond your means to sustain. Even when you are able to accept considerable risks of leverage, you still need to be judicious and take on only manageable risks.

One indicator that you should use in assessing your risk is your cash flow from a leveraged asset. Cash flow should be fairly strong and show a ratio to your equity investment that is above the rate of inflation. If the cash flow is small or neutral, you should be cautious, and if the cash flow is negative, you should walk away from the investment. The only reason you would want to buy the latter type of investment would be for speculation, and during your adulthood stage you should avoid speculation. It involves high economic risks, and it does not lead you to the kind of sustainable financial development that you need for your personal development during this stage of your life cycle.

Both Parties of a Household Should Work

The ways of the world are coming full circle. Two hundred years ago, when most people lived on the farm, men and women worked together with the chores of a farm. Women worked in the fields, driving horses and lifting bales of hay. Often women took over the full work of their husbands when they were sick or disabled. Our Victorian heritage gave us a role for women that was quite different, one that was removed from work, and at times almost fragile. Once again, women are becoming co-workers with men, as a growing number of women enter the work force. There are now increasing numbers of women who provide the principal income for their families.

All persons in their adulthood stage should spend some part of their time actively engaged in the business world. Since women have been mostly affected by the trend away from the home to the work force, this discussion largely pertains to them.

Providing a service to the commercial world, whether as a secretary, or as the chairman of the board, requires performance in an acceptable manner. These standards of performance will give you a clear idea of the requirements of the business world and your experience will build your confidence to meet them. There is no volunteer experience that can substitute for a commercial experience, because volunteer work does not usually involve such stringent standards of performance.

One result of both spouses working is that spending decisions should be joint decisions, especially if the earnings of the spouses are not widely different. The old days, when a husband made a gift to his wife of a refrigerator or a vacation, are gone. Similarly, the old adage that all of a wife's earnings should be saved is also a way of the past. That arrangement encouraged a sense of financial dominance of men over women that is no longer appropriate.

Having both spouses work provides, of course, a larger income than if only one person worked, and this additional income is valuable to a couple in their adulthood period. But the greater value of work is the education that it provides, laying the groundwork for opportunities for personal development in later stages of the life cycle. Many women in their subsequent midlife stage have a strong incentive to find work, and work would be a fine experience for them, but sometimes they do not succeed in this endeavor because they have little understanding of the rules of business life. The adulthood stage is the time to develop this understanding. At this period, you are flexible enough with the image you have of yourself to accommodate the sometimes rough but usually fair rules of the game of commercial work.

Develop an Entrepreneurial Skill

Most persons begin their careers as employees, not as entrepreneurs, who are people who run their own business. It is always easier to accept a job than to create a job. It is usually easier to continue to work as an employee than to take on the worries and risks of starting your own business. The principal reason many potential entrepreneurs never develop their own business is because they lack the experience of creating a job. In most cases they do not have a member of their family, close relative, or friend who is an entrepreneur, to whom they can turn for help and guidance.

Our schools and higher education systems do not provide this type of training. In fact, they provide training that prepares people for an employee status. In the transition from school to corporations or government, bosses are substituted for teachers, and position titles are substituted for grade levels. Yet the knowledge of an entrepreneur is essential if you are to fully achieve your potential self-development. You need to find out whether you have the skills that are required to run your own business. If you find the way of life of an entrepreneur to be excessively nerve-wracking and unsettling, you probably should be an employee. In fact, many employees make large amounts of money, as well as enjoy opportunities for personal development. The president of any major corporation is an employee, his income is high, and he is almost always regarded as a knowledgeable businessman.

Yet, some people would be more productive and develop themselves further if they were in business for themselves. These people, I have observed, tend to identify their goals and objectives personally. They are not content to turn over major profits from their work to the company that employs them in return for a salary, bonus, and possibly compliments. They believe that they deserve all profits from their work. Moreover, they tend to be independent in their thinking, and they usually find their position as an employee to be excessively confining.

You need to gain an insight into your abilities as an employee and as an entrepreneur. Almost everybody begins a working career as an employee. Then, year by year, a certain proportion step away from the employee status to start their own business. During your adulthood stage of the life cycle, you may take this step, and you will be strongly motivated to do so during your subsequent period, the midlife stage. Now is the time to develop some part-time experience as an entrepreneur or at least put your toe in the water, since this experience will become increasingly important as the years progress.

Make Friends Who Can Help You Develop Your Skills

As you settle into your work, you will soon find that certain people are leaders in your field. These people are regarded as the most reliable or most progressive or most competent. You should go to meetings where they speak and subscribe to magazines that feature their articles. You should meet these people and, possibly, write them a note about a subject that might be of mutual interest.

By taking these steps you are not embarrassing yourself or bothering these experts. Far from it. Most experts who are widely followed know very well how to control their communication with anybody but usually appreciate a brief note that might help them. This type of communication focuses your thinking and lets you relate your skills to persons who can give focus to your work. All of this takes considerable courage, since many people settle back with a moderate amount of contentment with their work in this stage of the life cycle. If you take this extra step, you will be doing your best to be sure that you complete the adulthood stage of your life cycle with flying colors.

KEY INCOME AND EXPENSE CATEGORIES

Savings

Savings can be regarded as having the same function for individuals as profit for a corporation. They represent a principal source of funds for the future development of a person or an organization. Savings provide the cushion against adversity and the basis for leverage, just as profits perform a similar function for a corporation.

You will keep your savings totals intact if you can at all do so. If unexpected expenses arise, such as the need to travel across the country to be with an ill parent, you should borrow rather than reduce your savings account. Many people find this to be shocking advice. "Why borrow," they ask, "when we have money sitting in the bank, and borrowing would require the payment of interest?" The answer is not financial but psychological. You will likely return the amount that you removed from your savings quicker if you borrow than if you draw down your savings account. The difference between your lost interest on a savings account and the interest expense of borrowing is not likely to be significant. The important point is that you would then be strongly motivated to replenish your savings reduction as quickly as possible. To do this, you would tend to be less generous in the way you spend your money for the other parts of your budget, and that self-discipline won't hurt a bit.

Your savings is your nest egg, and during the adulthood stage of your life cycle you should have a primary goal of building that nest egg. Your understanding of how you can build your savings represents the most important financial knowledge you can acquire during this period. This knowledge will be personal knowledge. You should learn how to control yourself and your spending habits to enable you to build your savings. Nobody can do this for you, and there are no rules of discipline that apply to everybody. You must learn these for yourself, because savings are the base on which you will build virtually every other financial accomplishment.

Housing

Perhaps no other part of your budget will be as difficult to put into practice as your spending for housing. You should not spend more than 30 percent of your combined family income for housing if you are buying a home, and about 20 percent if you are renting. The difference of 10 percent of your income between renting and buying should be put into some type of savings, so that you will be able to buy a home at some future date.

Some people in large cities may find this ratio of shelter spending to income to be too limiting. Many people believe that they should live in apartments they perceive to be in keeping with the stature of their work or their social standing. These apartments are often much more expensive than would be covered by the 20 percent guideline. Sometimes people who live in expensive metropolitan areas say to themselves that they should not be bound by a ratio that, they believe, pertains to people in other parts of the country.

There is no question that expensive apartments are pleasant places to live. But the financial issue at this stage of your life cycle is to find a way that you can eventually buy your first home. Unless you live in thrifty quarters and conserve your income, you may find yourself without the ability to buy a home or condominium if you should ever wish to do so. The willingness to live in less elegant surroundings in hopes of buying a home is one of the most common characteristics of people in their early years of the adulthood stage of the life cycle. Sometimes newly married couples deliberately choose an area that is inexpensive and rent minimal facilities as an incentive to move to their new home quickly.

The location of a home is particularly important at this stage of the life cycle. There are two rules that I have found to be important. First, you should try to live within walking distance of your work. Most Americans do not live close to their work, and it is difficult to want to live next to many heavy industries, such as refineries or steel mills. The principle applies if there are reasonably comfortable areas for housing nearby. The ability to walk to work gives you an enormous financial advantage of time over those who ride public transportation. A walk to work will give you perhaps one-half hour more time each day, compared with those who commute. That time can be used for your personal development or developing new skills. The money that does not go into transportation expense can be used to pay for personal development or can be added to your savings. And the exercise you get will contribute to your physical well-being.

Despite the many problems of home financing, there are many combinations of homeowner's work and financing that you may wish to explore. Sometimes you can buy a home that needs repairs by paying the seller a 5 or 10 percent bonus at the time of sale. You would also sign an agreement to accomplish certain repairs, such as installing a new roof or an upgraded kitchen. The owner would then give you 100 percent financing. The advantage to you is that you would be able to have the ownership of a home without a down payment. The seller would have the advantage of selling an unimproved home at full price. Moreover, if you did not fulfill your obligations of making regular payments on interest and principal to the seller, as well as upgrade the home along the lines of your agreement, the seller could repossess the property and likely have a better home than he sold.

The idea of a commute to work is typically American. Most communities in Europe and Asia have satisfactory housing in close proximity to working facilities. The cheapness of United States transportation and a desire to escape urban problems have combined to encourage the development of homes far from one's employment. But commuting is not good for your budget. If you do not like the housing that is located near your work, you may wish to change jobs. While you are in your adulthood stage, you can usually make such a change without financial penalty.

You should also consider the geographic area of the United States that appeals to you. Most people give an initial consideration to the area where they grew up. Some prefer to remain in that area, and others see a lure in some other area. Recently, the children of several friends have settled in the northern mountain states of Idaho and Wyoming, which is a type of migration that was unheard of 20 years ago. The ability to live more simply, live close to their work, and at a lower cost than in most other parts of the United States were keys to their decision.

The latter consideration is particularly important. Lower living costs bring lower income levels. But usually they bring lower taxes. Taxation is not a major issue in your adulthood stage, but it will become more important in later stages of the life cycle. Moreover, the tax burdens of major cities are going to be an increasingly heavy burden in future years. Many people prefer to live in major cities because of the commercial opportunities that large cities provide, and others prefer cities for their liberal culture. But large cities are no longer the only places that provide business opportunities, and the open-mindedness that attracted people to New York in the 1950s and to San Francisco in the 1960s has now spread among many other cities throughout the country.

One friend asked me which location in the United States offered the best commercial advantage to a young person who was indifferent to weather or the characteristics of any particular location. I suggested two cities that were still moderate sized and were sure to develop rapidly. The first was Nashville, Tennessee, which has been made a center of transportation by the interstate roads and has yet to develop fully into the commercial type of city that would be typical of a hub city. The second was San Jose, California, which is becoming the center for the rapidly growing semi-conductor and related electronics industries. There are also many other similar communities that have become a transportation focal point or are aligned to an emerging technology. In addition, there will be communities that may be designated as tax-free zones, and many of these communities will also provide business opportunities and pleasant living conditions.

Wages and Salary

Wages and salary are often regarded as being most important to a person in the adulthood stage of the life cycle. It seems as if everybody who enters the job market discusses his or her new job in terms of income. People with jobs that are high paying are automatically given top marks. The tendency to associate success with high income carries on throughout all of the subsequent stages of the life cycle.

Yet, during the adulthood stage, for both men and women, the tendency to seek high income could be a major mistake in managing your career and your money. Your personal talents may lie in a job that is not highly paid. This category includes most nonunionized crafts and trades as well as banking and retail selling. For example, you may have considerable interest and skill in library work or pottery making. Neither skill pays well to start. Yet, if you have talent, the income and prestige of being at the top of either of these fields is enormous. If you are discouraged by the low starting income, you may miss the right way to develop your inherent skills.

Moreover, your income is less imporant than your savings during this stage of your life cycle. I have observed that persons who stress their income often neglect their savings. For some reason of psychology that has never been explained to me, people who maintain high savings rates seldom discuss this talent. They typically build their savings in an inconspicuous manner. There is everything to benefit if you earn a large income and save a major portion of it. My experience, however, is that such a person is rare.

One friend illustrates the difference between income and savings rate. After completing college, he decided that he wanted to be completely self-sufficient, and with financial help from his family, purchased 14 acres of farm land in Florida. He lived in a shack until he sold his first crop and then took the profits to buy wood and roofing materials and built a garage. Step-by-step he became a farmer, starting with a small debt to his parents. His income was quite small, and each step of his investment was financed by savings.

I have always regarded this friend's experience as incredible. It clearly isn't typical of our current way of living. Yet, after World War II, people in the cities of Germany picked themselves up from the ashes and rebuilt their economy using exactly the same principle of a relatively high savings rate. It works.

Income Taxes

Income taxes are not critical to persons in the adulthood stage, although they will become important in subsequent stages of the life cycle. Until recently, the total effective tax rate has not been considered important to decisions concerning your location and the status of work. All of this has changed in the past few years, as inflation has pushed persons with ordinary income into moderately high incremental tax rates. As inflation continues and tax cuts lag the effects of inflation, taxes will become increasingly important to your financial and personal way of living.

The location of your work has an important bearing on your taxes. If you plan to live in a small community, you should plan to put down your roots early in your life cycle. People in small communities are trusted and usually are given informal advantages after they have been known over a period of years. In contrast, if you should decide to live in a large metropolitan city, your financial acceptance in the city is based largely on your financial statements. With city dwellers, there is no particular need to establish roots in one location.

The same standard of living, as measured in quantitative terms, will cost you much less in a small community than in a metropolitan city. For example, the difference between the cost of living in Boston and that of a small town in Texas is considerable. Your income in Boston must be considerably greater than double that of a small town simply to overcome the burden of higher tax rates as your income rises. The long-term tax impact of where you plan to live should be considered at this stage of your life cycle.

Another tax consideration is whether you plan to work as an employee or as an independent worker. There are marked tax benefits to being in business for yourself, as is discussed in a later stage of your life cycle. Nevertheless, a large number of people who subsequently open their own business gain experience as an employee during their adulthood stage. They obtain the educational benefits of being an employee in a leading organization and subsequently trade the security of being an employee for the potentially higher income and tax benefits of having their own business. It is helpful to have the tax benefits of an independent business in mind during employee status, to give perspective.

Life Insurance

This is the time to give careful consideration to life insurance. Perhaps no other use of money has become as controversial as life insurance in recent years. The idea of buying whole life insurance, particularly annuity insurance, has come under attack by a number of critics, because these types of insurance include both a coverage for the risk of death and the buildup of equity and cash as a form of savings. These critics show that this type of savings ordinarily yields significantly lower returns than are available elsewhere, and the difference, if compounded over a lifetime, can amount to a large sum of money.

These critics suggest that individuals should buy term insurance, since it is pure insurance. Term insurance is much less expensive than insurance that includes costs of a savings component. Term insurance, of course, rises in cost as you grow older and the term of coverage is renewed.

Agents of insurance companies have responded by asserting that there are advantages of forced savings that are often overlooked. These insurance agents take what they regard as a practical view of human nature and point out that many people have difficulty in maintaining a regular savings program. They suggest that these people are better served by a less efficient form of savings than little or no savings at all.

I have always believed that term life insurance is the proper type of insurance, because most people will follow a savings program if they have an incentive to do so. Nevertheless, when the flesh is weak and a person simply cannot resist the spending of the last dollar, possibly the last borrowed dollar, then there is a place for whole life insurance or even an endowment policy, which guarantees the accumulation of a certain sum by a future date. This type of policy should be taken out by someone who first of all recognizes his or her weakness, and knows that this type of forced savings is the best way to accumulate money.

There are a number of new approaches to life insurance that promise to make whole life insurance more competitive. A number of companies are now selling variable life insurance, in which the revenue from the insurance is invested in a managed common stock fund, a money market fund, and soon an equity real estate fund. This type of insurance has been sold in Great Britain and Europe for many years, and is likely to be an important new product in the United States.

The amount of life insurance you should carry at this stage of the life cycle should be sufficient to cover the expenses of your death, pay off your personal indebtedness, and enable those who presently rely on you to become self-sustaining. There are various other guidelines, such as the rule of thumb that your life insurance should amount to three times your annual income.

Despite the guidelines, the insurance needs of many men in the adulthood stage of the life cycle have actually declined in recent years as wives have joined the labor force in increasing numbers. These women need not actually have jobs to reduce a husband's insurance needs. If they have a commercial skill that can be used in the event of a husband's death, this potential support for the woman reduces a husband's needs for insurance. Nevertheless, this change in the working style of women has increased their insurance needs. If a family relies on the income of a working wife, she now needs insurance as much as her working husband. So the total insurance needs of a household may now be distributed differently than in the past.

It is just as much a mistake to be insurance rich as insurance poor. If you carry too much life insurance, the cost of this insurance reduces money that would be available for savings and consumption. That represents a loss that is little different than a situation in which insurance cannot cover basic needs.

After you have determined your insurance needs, you should shop for the best rates available. You should contact several independent insurance agents and ask them to give you quotes for the exact insurance coverage you request. You should select independent agents who sell the insurance of many companies, because these agents are the only ones who represent more than one company and can give you competitive quotes. You should contact several of these independent agents so that you can compare their results and services.

One friend carried this effort to compare companies to a considerable length. She wrote a letter to five independent agents and 20 insurance companies and asked them for the insurance she felt that she needed. She also requested that these agents and companies respond by letter and specifically asked them not to phone her. The results showed a 20 percent variation in premiums between the high and low offers.

Insurance is perhaps the most completely regulated industry in America. Because of complicated accounting, the differences in quality of insuring companies are virtually impossible for the layman to figure out. Thus the average person cannot make an objective case for buying insurance from one company compared with another on the basis of differences in the quality of the companies. Price and service distinguish one company from another.

Several years ago, a friend who is in the insurance business shopped for insurance in the United States, Canada, and Switzerland, and found lower premiums in the latter two countries. The lower premiums reflected, in part, a longer life expectancy in those countries than in the state from which he was applying. He had relatives in both countries and was able to establish communication with local agents of insurance companies. He added an additional factor to his evaluation by considering the long-term changes in the value of the United States dollar compared with the Canadian dollar or the Swiss franc. If the changes in value of these currencies are gradual, differences in value of premiums will broadly match differences in the value of coverage. In other words, if the value of the Swiss franc slowly rises, he will be gradually paying more dollars for his coverage, but his coverage will also be rising proportionately. This person bought the foreign-based insurance, and his heirs will collect on this policy abroad.

KEY ASSETS AND LIABILITIES

Housing

The conventional wisdom since World War II has been to buy a house, particularly during the adulthood stage years.

The increase in housing prices during most of those post-war years, and the underlying expectations of further inflation, have encouraged most people to believe that house prices are destined to rise for as far ahead as they can see. It has also led to the belief that there is virtually no financial risk in purchasing a house.

The price appreciation of home ownership has been a windfall to persons who have worked in industrial areas. When these people have retired, they have often sold their homes at a high price and have moved to lower cost homes in warmer parts of the country. Through an exemption in taxes for retired persons who sell their homes, this transaction has often given those people tens of thousands of dollars in cash to enjoy during their retirement years. With experiences like these, which regularly have occurred in virtually all families, it is no wonder that persons in their adulthood years are ready to take major personal sacrifices to buy a home.

The key to the attractiveness of housing is the leverage lending institutions provide. Most people have borrowed 80 to 90 percent of the cost of a home. No other major investment is so highly leveraged on so wide a scale. The advantage of this leverage has been enormous, since it has allowed a relatively small amount of equity to reap the benefits of a major rise in the value of homes. There is an additional benefit to this leverage, since the servicing costs of the borrowed money are deductible from income taxes. On an after-tax basis, the servicing expense of buying a home is often cut by one-third or one-half, since the marginal tax rate of many families is now well above 30 percent. The rate of inflation in recent years has been as high as the remaining after-tax cost of borrowing. Thus, many home buyers have found that on this adjusted basis, their borrowing costs literally disappear, as the value of their houses climbed upward.

There have been, at various times, dips in real estate prices. But these declines have been temporary in post-war years. For example, California real estate prices declined almost 20 percent from 1957 to 1962. During that five-year period there were many worried homeowners who had to sell their property. These sellers lost money on their homes. The recovery in home prices of the latter half of the 1960s and the explosion in real estate prices of the 1970s made California homes the most expensive in the nation.

There has even been a turnaround in real estate prices in many central cities during the past decade. Investors have refurbished those residences and the rise in gasoline and transportation costs have attracted many buyers to this type of location. One couple purchased a home in the central part of Washington, D.C. and spent twice their purchase cost in renovations. After living in the home for three years, they sold the home for double their costs of purchase and renovation.

Despite this record of overall success, there are warning flags flying in the real estate market. Homes in many areas of the country have become so expensive that families typically need two incomes to afford them. And in many of these instances, homeownership costs account for more than one-third of a family's budget. That development has a double-edged effect. Fewer families are able to afford a home as the proportion of home-ownership costs rise. That trend acts as a damper to home purchases. However, there is now an incentive for families to buy homes simply to get into the housing market. This development of strong counterforces makes the housing market increasingly fragile. Any protracted decline in housing prices would reduce the demand of buyers who would be willing to undertake major financial sacrifices to buy a home. The removal of this source of buyers could bring about a drop in home prices.

The price of homes in many parts of the country has now reached a point where it fails a basic economic test of investment. The price of an asset should be related to its ability to generate sufficient income to cover costs. The cost of financing a home is now two to three times greater than its rental income. For example, in many parts of the country a home that costs $1,500 per month in payments to cover principal, interest, insurance, and taxes receives rental income of only $500 to $700 per month. In this analysis, maintenance costs are assumed to offset principal payments, and the real estate is kept in good repair. Moreover, the price of homes in many areas of the country have increased to levels that, by comparative standards, are much above that of other assets. Thus many home prices may have reached a speculative level, with prices based on belief that somebody else will be willing to pay more for the home than was paid in the last transaction.

A person in the adulthood stage of his or her life cycle is thus caught in a difficult financial decision concerning the purchase of a home. Despite the high prices of houses and questions concerning the future direction of real estate prices, a person in this stage of the life cycle should plan to buy a home. A home is a major emotional issue as well as a major financial issue. It reflects the interest of a person in this stage to put down roots. This emotional need is more important than the financial aspects of trying to outguess the direction of real estate prices.

Nevertheless, there are several ways the possible risks of real estate may be minimized. As mentioned, one approach is to buy a home within walking distance of work. The cost of commuting has risen sharply, and home prices in many areas still have not caught up with the implications of this change. The ability to cut a major portion of transportation costs represents a partial offset to high home costs. In another instance, persons who are adventuresome and handy with tools may see a future in rehabilitating a home in an old area. Special low-interest government loans are often available through banks and savings and loan associations, and the loans have the effect of further reducing the price of these homes. A new approach is equity sharing, which has grown rapidly in many parts of the country where real estate prices have risen rapidly. In this arrangement, a home owner and an investor form a partnership and share in changes in the value of the real estate.

Persons who tackle their home needs by this approach need to have a pioneering spirit. They need to believe that they are the leading edge of civilization in a difficult and sometimes hostile land. In earlier times, pioneers faced attacks from Indian tribes, fires, and a lack of the services of an established community. Today, many parts of cities are no different. Crime and violence may come from drug addicts rather than from Indians. Fires and riots can occur and a sense of community may be missing, even though many persons are located closely together. The quest to develop something of value from a hostile environment is still the sustaining force of a pioneer. Perhaps little has changed for this type of person in the past two centuries, except in the location of the frontier.

There is always the possibility that you will find a home that has been decorated in a way that is not regarded as attractive by most people, and this house may be an opportunity. Many homes built in the 1940s and early 1950s may be decorated in the dark greens and browns that were popular in that era. A realtor told me that a coat of white paint quickly makes these homes more appealing. If you see a darkly painted home and it otherwise fulfills your needs, you may be able to buy it at a price under the price that it would fetch, if it were decorated to today's taste.

Some people prefer to rent for a variety of reasons. They may expect to move in the near future, they may be concerned about what they regard as excessively high prices of real estate in a favorite area, they may not like the responsibilities of home ownership, or they may not have enough money for a down payment on a home. One way of taking a position in real estate but not owning a home is to buy a share in a limited partnership of a real estate parcel, such as an apartment or a commercial building. Most realtors of these partnerships can provide you with a selection. You should be careful about the legal and tax issues of these partnerships and buy them only after you have paid a lawyer and an accountant for a review.

Stocks and Bonds

As the real estate market has boomed in the past decade, the stock and bond markets have declined. Many persons in the adulthood stage of their life cycle have avoided securities simply because their performance has been so poor.

Nevertheless, the drawback to securities in this stage of your life cycle is not their performance, but is your lack of experience in these markets. Most investors in the adulthood stage are either too trusting or too skeptical. They have not had enough experience to look at the shades of gray that are a part of all investments, and to make decisions that are based on facts that are only partially known. Securities are intangible, but a home or car is tangible and controllable. Everybody can recognize a squeaky floor, but not everyone understands how to measure the impact of a low quick-cash position on a corporate security.

Still, there is no substitute for experience as a teacher. You should hold a relatively small amount of your assets in securities, and you should regard the experience as part of your education. At a later period in your life cycle you will want to hold a larger portion of your assets in securities, and the experience in securities that you gather during your adulthood stage will be valuable to you then.

Bank Loans and Deposits

During your adulthood stage you will want to have a record of both loans and deposits in a bank. You may also wish to have loans or deposits with savings and loan associations and credit unions. But banks are your target financial institutions, because among all types of financial institutions, they alone have the ability to make loans for virtually any purpose.

The purpose of simultaneously borrowing and depositing with a bank is to establish a business relationship with the bank. You are now laying the foundation for your credit standing, and the more information a bank has about the way you handle your money, the better will be your position when you should someday approach the bank for a major commercial loan. That time will likely occur during a later stage of your life cycle. The adulthood stage is the period when you lay the groundwork for that loan and establish a steady record of creditworthiness.

Of course, you should not borrow unnecessarily. But most people borrow money, some frequently, during their adulthood stage. The best approach to short-term borrowing is to request an instant loan arrangement with your checking account from your bank. Then, as you alternatively use the loan portion and pay it off, you will establish the record of being able to control your credit lines by yourself. In so doing, you will build a financial history that will tell your bank that you can handle credit, and that you fully understand the rules about the repayment of debts. This record, with its implications for future borrowing, are worth more money than you could ever save in a lifetime.

A Secondary Business

During the adulthood stage most persons are fully occupied with their regular work and family and have virtually no time for hobbies or a side business. This is a serious shortsight, since you need to keep some breadth to your interests. You will need this breadth of vision in your next stage of the life cycle. It is always better to develop breadth to your business experience than suddenly to try to develop it.

Some persons keep their breadth of vision alive through their hobbies. These hobbies include some of the literally thousands of activities from gardening, hunting, and dollhouse building to ex libris collecting. I am always amazed at the variety of hobbies in the world, especially in England and the United States, and the organizations, magazines, and meetings that serve the hobbies.

Hobbies are important during the adulthood stage of the life cycle. Activities that serve as hobbies should be taken one step further and be used as the basis of a small side business. The line between a hobby and a side business is not wide, but it does involve the additional emphasis of developing the hobby as a personal interest as well as a commercial venture. Most people enjoy the added opportunities that a commercial venture brings.

A small side business could become valuable to you at some future time. Most side businesses do not generate enough volume or profit to be attractive for somebody to buy. Yet a small personal business is the nucleus of a possible future business. That germ of an idea has value to you.

One friend enjoyed working with bicycles in his spare time. His regular work was as an electrical engineer for an aerospace company. Over a period of years he developed a small business in repairing bicycles. He built several high-quality sports bicycles for competition which were well received by racing cyclists. When he was laid off work, this side business provided him with a supplemental income, and most importantly, kept his mind engaged in work he enjoyed. Seven months later a bicycle shop in his neighborhood became available. He bought the shop, and because of the high-quality repair service he offered, this shop is now one of the most profitable in the area.

Side businesses are often a truer reflection of a person's interests and abilities than his or her full-time work. When career difficulties occur, persons with strong hobbies or small businesses tend to bounce back quickly. They tend to use the adversity as a stepping stone to a much stronger understanding of themselves and their work. Some persons continue their hobbies or side businesses throughout their lifetime without any other use. Nevertheless, a side business represents a personal reservoir of interest that extends beyond your immediate career, and the adulthood stage is the time this should be initially developed.

Will

A will is an essential part of your financial package in this stage of the life cycle. You may think that it is premature to prepare a will, since most persons in their adulthood stage enjoy good health. But there are exceptions. The law is designed to handle your estate quickly and economically, but only if you leave this world with a will. Your loved ones deserve to receive your possessions quickly once you pass away. If you do not have a will, this may not happen, and if your assets are large, it clearly won't happen.

A will is a statement of wishes you want carried out after you die. It should be written in correct legal language. Most lawyers charge a nominal fee for simple wills, and it is worth the fee to obtain a lawyer's services. Be sure to ask what the legal charge will be for a will when you begin discussions. If you believe that the fee is excessive, look for another lawyer.

The major roadblock to making a will for most persons is not a lack of funds but an unwillingness to face the idea that they will inevitably die. You may not like to think about a will during your adulthood period, but you should. It is a step that takes a bit of hard-minded thinking to accomplish, but once done, can be forgotten in good conscience.

Chapter 9

THE MIDLIFE
CHALLENGE:
AGE 36 TO 50

*T*HE midlife challenge represents a peak experience. It is
a stage in your life cycle when you will be challenged more by
yourself than at any other period. During your earlier period
of challenge, adolescence, you did not have the experience to
use as your raw material to develop. You had not developed
the uniqueness that you now have acquired. During a later
period of challenge, age and simplicity, you will not have the
energy to see your efforts through to completion as you have
in midlife. Never before and never again will you have the
combination of such mastery of skills and be endowed with
abundant vitality.

This stage of the life cycle is often referred to as the period
of midlife crisis. There is, of course, an element of crisis in
this period, where opportunity and danger coexist and sometimes appear indistinguishable. But the period should be
regarded as being more of a challenge than a crisis. It is the

positive emphasis which challenge implies that makes this stage of the life cycle so important.

The midlife challenge is the period when you ask again all of the basic questions of your life. It is as if you place yourself under the harsh lights of self-examination and question every part of your identity. You seek to find your true nature. Wherever you find aspects of your work or your relationships with others that do not fit this nature, you challenge, criticize, and rebel.

This winnowing process is not basically destructive. Although it forces you to let loose whatever hopes and dreams you really don't believe in, it focuses thought and action to the center of your individuality. The effect is not to expunge your individuality, rather, it is to emphasize it. The parts of your innermost being that are not really characteristic of you are challenged, and only your truest, most indigenous aspects emerge from the test unscathed.

Challenges require an arbiter. Someone is needed to determine whether challenges have been met successfully. You must act as your own arbiter, and this is a time when it is impossible to cheat or pretend. Persons who have focused on their strengths and fully reflect who they are find an enormous energy to fulfill their days. Persons who do not succeed in this challenge usually find their energies are blocked by doubts, hesitations, and uncertainties of whether they are pursuing the right course.

The midlife period of the life cycle is the period when we take steps to become more clearly who we really are. In the adulthood stage of the life cycle you imitated more than you searched for yourself. Yet, there is a time to stop apprenticing and test what you have learned. We are not copies of others, we are only partially a reflection of our family, friends, and culture. Each of us is unique, and the midlife challenge is perhaps the most important time of our life to focus on our uniqueness.

It is the destruction of our mentors as leaders that usually ushers in the midlife challenge. The person who counseled us in a career or who has helped in a club or church or who was a guiding friend, now no longer has the charisma that he or she held before. In the midlife stage, you see this person with feet of clay, with imperfections and shortcomings. You shift your focus from being a docile pupil to that of the doer. You no longer want to learn from others so much as you want to be the focus of activity. Unlike the adolescent stage of the life cycle, the challenge is not with people and things, but the challenge is in the mind. The search is for an inner identity.

There is no way of measuring success externally in this stage of the life cycle. The amount of income, or your standard of living misses the point. There are no statistics, no financial or other data that would serve as an objective guide, as was the case with the adulthood stage.

The test of success in this stage is measured inwardly. Persons who find the midlife challenge to be invigorating and liberating have tended to be the ones who lay the plans and the foundations for their subsequent success in the maturity stage of the life cycle. They feel strengthened by their greater insights of themselves, and they are pleased with the person whom they perceive more clearly as themselves.

The converse also appears to apply. Persons who regard the midlife stage as an unhappy period usually find the further process of self-discovery to be upsetting. They regret that the relative calm of an earlier stage of the life cycle has passed. These persons sometimes rebel against their friends and former loved ones. However, the rebellion is not against others, it is really against themselves. These persons find the challenge of the midlife stage to be a shattering experience. Instead of finding their insights into themselves liberating, they find them to be frightening. They are not willing to let go of the image they have accepted from their family and friends of an earlier stage. Instead of casting off the image that is less accurate of them, they cling, sometimes desperately, to the old image. The truth about themselves scares them.

These persons are under considerable tension between urges to develop their individual nature and restraint to block this development. That strain exacts a toll. It is difficult to accomplish much when the mind is under tension. The longing for an earlier period represents a wish that the challenge and inner energy of this stage would go away. These persons usually accomplish much less in subsequent stages of the life cycle than persons who are able to use their energies constructively.

One friend, who is one of the most accomplished accountants I know, worked in a large insurance company and was given responsibility to solve problems that nobody else could solve. He would regularly take the most obscure clues and use them in an imaginative and clever manner to solve a wide range of financial problems. Despite this intellectual ability, he never was able to impress his associates that he possessed much management ability. In his midlife period he often became emotional over issues that seemed trivial to persons around him. These outbursts probably indicated an effort to assert himself. I believe that these efforts failed to achieve their purpose of freeing him from his didactic manner, because he never developed the expressive side of his nature, and he was unwilling to let go of the iron-clad control in which he held himself. He apparently feared a loss of finely tuned intellectual ability, and he probably felt that the development of a more amiable manner would ruin his mind. Of course, nothing like that would have happened. But this fear kept him in the prison of his past.

Another friend had spent 16 years in the securities business. After beginning his career in a large national organization, he rose rapidly from research to retail sales to institutional sales. He then joined an elite regional firm and found that his hard work and attentive manner no longer won him the promotions they had with the national firm. He was not accepted because he did not have an Ivy League background, to which most of the partners of the firm belonged. The regional firm was then sold to an even more exclusive firm, and at the age of 40, he decided to strike out in business for himself.

His first venture was to open an antique auction. This effort proved to be disappointing, and he then attempted to buy a retail home supply company, mostly on credit. He ran out of money and reluctantly returned to a major institutional securities firm, where he quickly regained his leadership as a highly successful salesman.

This person's effort to start his own business was not a mistake. In both attempts at starting his own business he was asserting that he did not wish to be an employee and was seeking a way of avoiding this way of working. This kind of personal assertion is common during the period of the midlife challenge. I would expect that this person will build up his assets and try to develop his own business again, this time with more capital.

The midlife challenge has a particularly strong impact on women. Many women are now setting a standard for themselves that is more strenuous and challenging than that of men. As a result, the midlife challenge is now affecting large numbers of women in a new way, and placing strains on these women that they find difficult to resolve.

It is no accident that the divorce rate is high in the midlife stage of the life cycle. In past generations the stress men faced in this period was usually soothed by wives. Women have always been faced with the unsettling effects of the midlife stage, but in the past they regarded their role primarily to be supportive of their husbands. The change that has occurred in the role of women has placed considerable stress on marriages. Many wives now feel overwhelmed by the dual responsibilities of being wives and pursuing personal self-fulfillment. Sometimes they feel that they must choose between the two roles, and the role of wife is not as important as what they regard as their personal self-fulfillment. Often, this dilemma leads to divorce.

One couple faced this problem in an accommodative way. The wife embarked on a strenuous three-year law course. Her husband was a medical doctor and had some flexibility in his hours. Nevertheless, the family, which included two children in their early teens, needed to cooperate in sharing tasks that ordinarily would have been provided by the wife. The period of change in this family's life was certain to be long-range.

The strain of law school would be replaced by the strain of legal practice. Nevertheless, the program worked. The family is together and has weathered the strain. I think that the principal reason this effort was a success was the honesty with which both husband and wife faced the implications of the wife's challenge. The sacrifices were understood and knowingly made. I also believe that there was a deep love for each other, which formed the basis of the sacrifice.

It is really not satisfactory to suggest that the alternative for this family would have been for the wife to have continued her role as being exclusively mother and wife. That role would have been unsatisfactory for her, and she would have sought some other vehicle for her self-fulfillment. She felt that she had to assume a personal role beyond that of being a wife, and it would have been difficult for her to accept a role that did not serve that challenge.

Sometimes divorce is the best solution to the realization that a husband and wife are moving in different directions. The key is whether the directions are compatible. Most often the directions are compatible, but one of the partners believes that the other is not interesting any longer. That is an issue that moves beyond what can be answered objectively. As unpleasant an experience as it is, divorce does provide a way of clearing the decks and starting anew, and there is a strong incentive to respond to a new start in your personal life during the midlife stage of the life cycle. But you need to be certain that your sights are as clear as possible before you begin a divorce, because it often adds strain, rather than lessens it.

Not all efforts of women to move beyond their homes are successful. Another friend who was the wife of a rising tax accountant was very conscious of status and social position. She looked on the work of a secretary as being somewhat demeaning, although it was the most senior work she was qualified to do.

She looked for work in keeping with her image and found a position that was titled "special assistant to the manager" of a fashionable club. She had hoped that her title and association with a prestigious club would elevate her status as an employee. The work in the club really was not as elevated as the title of the job indicated. She was simply the secretary to the club manager. There was no glamor, only lots of work. She left the job after four months.

This person began facing an aspect of the midlife challenge in a typical way. At her first job she believed that her fantasies could be made real. She had not looked at either herself or the work that she could perform in a realistic manner. The role of being a clubwoman probably would not have satisfied her needs for identity, even if the job with the club had fitted her original hopes. Moreover, she had not resolved the question of whether she was willing to make the personal sacrifices that any job requires.

Another friend never married and was deeply depressed by this fact as her midlife stage unfolded. She had been educated at an excellent women's college and had worked for more than fifteen years in a major corporation. She had risen to successively higher positions in the bank, and at age 40 she was in charge of a group of over 100 persons, most of whom were skilled technicians.

Her work hours increased, and her dedication to her job became an obsession. Often she spent late evenings and weekends working on what she perceived as the assignment that would be the next rung up the ladder of advancement in the corporation.

As the quantity of the hours of her work increased, her effectiveness dropped. The volume of work her group produced was prodigious. Yet no one understood their results. Nevertheless, they admired the technical skill she and her group displayed. But her insight into what needed to be accomplished seemed to fail her. Her mistakes were not technical, they were mistakes concerning the way people in the organization thought and acted. She did not understand how to make her techinical programs useful to people who had other interests besides technical results.

The midlife stage of the life cycle gave her a second chance at adolescence. It gave her another opportunity to see herself in a candid way, and in fact, forced her to do so. But she avoided that insight, and resumed her work with even more dedication than before. Yet, she failed, because a part of her was again pushed into the shadow. If this shadow side of her could have developed, she would have become more successful in her work, as well as a more complete person.

Not everybody can develop into what is described as a balanced person, and probably not everybody should try to do so. The world is full of people who lack complete integration in one way or another. Yet the challenge of trying to see how complete one can become is another matter. The challenge forces us to seek our limits, to stretch our understanding to its limit. This effort always leaves its mark for our benefit, regardless of how we eventually settle with ourselves. The challenge of midlife makes us more sensitive to ourselves and gives us a wider understanding of what our real strengths are and where our limitations lie. We don't become different persons, we become more finely etched persons, with greater clarity.

Sometimes the midlife challenge becomes overwhelming, and the person loses his or her sense of identity for a while. The sense of being lost is often a result of an incessant selfexamination that never gives an inch. The search can provide so much light that it blinds and burns, leaving more destroyed than revealed.

One friend was married to a businessman who was suddenly fired during a business recession. Their lives had previously been centered around the corporation he worked for and their family. The loss of her husband's job occurred as she was becoming intrigued with Far-Eastern religions. At first she tried to give her husband moral support in his efforts to find new work. As the weeks turned into months, she withdrew from her husband's and her family's problems and focused her attention entirely on her own challenge of identity. She sought to purge herself of ideas that she felt were not truly hers. Marriage involves an enormous amount of accommodation, and as many people have remarked, a happy old couple actually looks alike. She began to believe that any help for her husband would cause her to be a failure. The strain became enormous, and the couple divorced.

Faced with the prospect of a small alimony, she looked for work. Her first job was selling furniture at a design studio. Her artistic introspection clashed with the requirement to get customers to buy, and this work didn't prove enlightening or profitable. I had noticed through the years that she had shown fine dexterity in serving food as well as an almost overpowering interest in health. I remarked to her that she had never developed the skills in her hands, and that this skill must give her pleasure because she was so good at it. If she could combine that skill with work in the health field, she might be surprised at the result.

One year after making the suggestion, she enrolled in a dental hygiene training progam, graduated with honors, and now is one of the most sought dental hygienists in her community. She combines her skill with a particularly pleasing manner. She found a way of combining two personal needs which seemed quite unrelated into work that has given her a new meaning.

All of the trauma which often accompanies the midlife stage of the life cycle may not be completely necessary. Was it necessary, in the above example, for a person to suffer such personal torments that she disappeared from her family in spirit, divorced her husband, and lived under financial hardship for several years? The other side of that question is whether an accommodating and supportive spouse, parents, or friends could not have helped work out the final solution earlier and saved the turmoil and stress. One answer is that turmoil and stress are essential to the development of the person. Moreover, what appears as stress to others is perceived by the person undergoing this stage of the life cycle as an exciting journey, full of wonderful or dangerously interesting insights. The stress is actually sought as part of the process of self-fulfillment.

I don't completely agree with this point of view. There are too many ways people can damage themselves, and others, not to seek ways that the stress of the midlife challenge can be kept at lower levels of intensity. It is possible to accomplish the personal benefits of this stage of the life cycle with more moderate stress and tension.

The sense of isolation that is so frequently felt in the midlife stage should be offset by the company of someone who has a fullness of life and a warmth of character. The midlife stage can become so introspective that a person literally can cut himself or herself off from the important learning experiences of other people. The best way to journey through the midlife years is to do so with at least one close friend who makes you glad to be alive. You won't miss the introspection that is a key part of this period, but you will probably keep your sense of balance better, and use your discoveries about yourself more meaningfully.

One aspect of the midlife stage of the life cycle is its retrospective direction. Many people focus on their parents and their childhood hobbies. Some persons imagine conversations in a youthful setting with their mother and father, as well as imagine youthful activities, their hobbies, and chores. These flights of the imagination are some of the most powerful stimuli that a person can experience.

The thought of a conversation with a parent 30 years in the past with a consciousness that is 30 years further developed is a challenging feat of the mind. In this image, the child possesses the same power of understanding as a parent and is not in a subservient position. It is as if we could go back and see our parents as adults, not as fathers and mothers. People who have mentioned this fantasy have always said how liberating the experience has been. Even persons who recall their parents as being difficult and overbearing sense that whatever the reason for this difficult relationship, they can now see their parents simply as people.

The second look into the past is the focus on hobbies or toys. It is as if our inner interests are more clearly revealed in childhood, and as we grow up, we adapt our interests to the hopes of parents, encouragement of teachers, and strivings of our peer group. The toys of the child, as Eric Erickson points out, are the theories of the old man. Hobbies are the key to the growth of the inner talents of a person. They represent what we would do all of our lives, if our work were to give us a full measure of enjoyment.

As we think of our hobbies in this stage of the life cycle, we are often rejuvenated. By looking back to our childhood, we see again with clarity the simple activities which give us pleasure. That is a great feat. If we have strayed from our basic interests, we can catch a glimpse of our true interests once again. If we have pursued these interests, reminiscing about our early hobbies gives us the satisfaction of seeing how we have developed and how well we have lived up to our promise. It is our hobbies that keep our true feelings about work alive, and if hobbies are retained, they provide an enormous benefit to the challenges of the midlife stage of the life cycle.

The midlife period challenges both our personal lives and our working lives. It is probably more important to resolve the challenges of our personal lives than our work lives. People who resolve their personal challenges have almost always been able to meet their work challenges favorably, but the reverse often does not work out so well. The source of our deepest strength during the midlife stage is our personal identity, and our loved ones give us a better reflection of that identity than our working associates.

The ability to see ourselves as we really are is not usually fostered in business situations. Nevertheless, the majority of the most successful businesspeople I have known, usually presidents or chairmen of their companies or outstanding salespeople, have developed this sense of identity. These people have caught an understanding of who they are and what their limits are, and they quickly guide you to their strengths. Their business rewards are really extensions of the inner direction they have developed. They are successful because they have developed their identity.

The unhappiness with one's career is a common complaint among people during this stage of the life cycle. The malaise is particularly strong among men who attended prestigious colleges and joined companies that have names that are highly regarded. By the time a man is 45 years of age, has worked hard for his company, and has perhaps been promoted to a vice president, he would ordinarily be expected to be proud of his position. Nevertheless, I have yet to meet a happy person in this situation. Many of these men regard their corporate position as mediocre, and some regard it as being hollow. Virtually all these persons have sacrificed their lives on the altar of ambition. They have given their corporate job their full devotion, and whenever there has been a conflict with their family, usually it has been their family that suffered.

One friend graduated near the top of his class from an Ivy League business school. He had risen to the position of senior vice president of marketing of a major conglomerate corporation. When I last visited him in his office in New York, he looked more agitated than dynamic. I felt that something was wrong and said so. He looked at me, almost with a glare in his eyes that I should ask such a personal question in what was obviously a large and impressive office. He turned on a tape recorder that sounded much like waves on a beach, and explained that the machine played a type of sound that made it impossible to tape conversations. He said that he was concerned that his company might be checking on him, and he didn't want them to know how unhappy he was or they would fire him.

I was struck with how this person's technical success as an outstanding marketing executive really meant little to him. I told him that I would have been proud to have his marketing successes. His response was that those successes meant little to him because he had not achieved what he really wanted. He had allowed himself to become a prisoner of success and didn't know how to get out of it. His deep dissatisfaction with his life reflected the stirrings of the midlife challenge, and I would expect that this person would either leave his job and quit all work for possibly a year or leave his wife. If he were wise, he would leave his job and with his wife build his ideas of himself and his talents from scratch.

One of the common characteristics of persons who seem to surmount the midlife challenge successfully is that they become their own bosses. These persons take a fundamental shift in the focus of their career. They turn away from being specialists to take on the broader responsibilities of being responsible for other persons. They respond to the midlife challenge by turning away from the sources of their earlier success, which involved increasing proficiency at their specialties, and begin to manage people. These are tasks for which they had not trained, since the responsibility of the other persons is not a job for a specialist.

These people tend to be at the upper age of the midlife stage, and they worry less about themselves than other people. Not all of these persons are in business. Some continued to practice their specialties and professions.

Nevertheless, it is in business that this shift is most obvious. Only a few of these persons were promoted to the presidencies of their companies. That is easy to understand. There is room for only one president in any company, and the chances of becoming president of one of the large corporations that employ thousands of persons is remote, even for a gifted and qualified person. The pyramid of progression is brutal and allows no real substitute for leadership for those who are a rung below the top.

What is most interesting is how talented persons face this challenge. The choice of remaining inside the corporation is a safe one, but it involves a relatively low chance of becoming one's own boss. Many persons who remain within a large corporation do, in fact, harbor the hope that they will be chosen, and they secretly believe that in the end, they will be given the role of being their own boss. Yet I also believe that these persons are also fearful of failing, if they should leave their corporation. Many have built up long-standing friendships within their companies, and they question how effective they would be without those friendships. Others are not sure they could withstand the long hours and financial worries that they might face if they left their companies and joined a different company for a top position that did not work out.

The other choice of the challenge of becoming one's own boss is to start a business. This is a difficult choice for many businesspeople who are well established in their companies. A new business always involves more work, more trouble, and less financial security than before. Yet, it is often the right solution for persons who have the talent to lead but will never be able to do so as intermediate or even an upper-level official of a large company.

The resolution of the challenge of midlife involves the development of new clarity in your identity. The process involves a need for being honest about everything. You also need the focus of leadership to give you the means of fulfilling the promise of which the midlife stage gives you a glimpse. This fulfillment will come in the next stage of the life cycle, when you pass along the torch of your knowledge. If you don't find a way of practicing leadership, you won't receive the satisfaction that is inherent in this next stage, and you will likely fall back into a more narrow life of specialization. If you find a way of using your leadership, you will look back at the midlife challenge as the best years of all.

Chapter 10

THE FINANCIAL STRATEGY OF MIDLIFE: FINANCING THE NEW DEVELOPMENT OF YOUR TALENT

*T*HIS is the period when your search for self-identity again becomes as important as it was during your adolescence stage. This time your search involves an inner discovery of the uniqueness of yourself. Your exploration will require money. Some part of the savings and assets you have built up during your adulthood stage may be spent at this time, either by the liquidation of some of your assets or by borrowing against them.

There are five important financial strategies for the mid-life period of the life cycle: (1) liquidity is essential, (2) keep personal living expenses low, (3) spend money for new insights, (4) prepare a five-year life plan, and (5) look at the tax consequence of your life plan.

The midlife period is a time when you make mistakes, and you may appear to waste money. This is to be expected, since any exploration involves mistakes and wasted efforts, when viewed in retrospect. But at the time of the exploration, these mistakes are an essential part of your discovery. No one ever moved in a straight line in the discovery of anything. You should not worry about the cost of these mistakes. Nevertheless, your financial problems are likely to be resolved more smoothly if you build up funds in the earlier stage of the life cycle.

You may have an impression that your finances are not as much under your control as during the previous stage of your life cycle. You may even feel that you are slipping in your ability to handle your money. Don't worry. You will regain a grip on your spending during the next stage. That stage is the maturity period, when you consolidate the discoveries you make during your midlife period. At that future time you will draw together your new insights, distill them, and organize them in a powerful way.

The strength of that future consolidation will reflect, in a large part, the variety and abundance of the raw material that you develop during your midlife stage. The deeper the insights and the richer the material about yourself, the finer will be the subsequent amalgam. Thus you should not worry if your finances appear chaotic during your midlife stage. You should be primarily concerned that you are using your money as creatively as possible.

KEY FINANCIAL GOALS OF MIDLIFE

Liquidity Is Essential

This is the time to make new financial investments as liquid as possible. You may even wish to convert some of your investments from an earlier stage of your life cycle into liquid assets, if your assets include a particularly large proportion of illiquid assets such as property holdings. Of course, if these assets are important to your work or if their liquidation would involve a major tax liability, it may be better to hold them without change.

The emphasis during the midlife stage of your life cycle is to have your funds ready to use. For example, if your personal interests should lead you to want to open a store, the mortgage and ownership of 30 acres of vacant land would not be of much help in the financing. Even during periods of slack loan demand, commercial lenders avoid making loans against undeveloped land.

To further expand your liquidity, you should open a line of credit with a bank and seek the maximum line available. You may never use this line of credit, but it could provide you with an extra dimension of funds, should an occasion arise when you would need cash quickly. More importantly, the application for a personal line of credit will give you a measure of your borrowing capacity before you need it. You need to know the extent of your financial limits, because you may wish to stretch these limits in the process of your personal or career development.

Keep Personal Living Expenses Low

You should be frugal with living expenses in this period, because you should transfer part of your consumption expenses to your personal development spending, in order to provide for the expansion of those areas of activity. At first, this change in your budget may appear to be a difficult task, particularly if you work for a major company and you have tied your business image to conspicuous consumption. But you may be a bit weary of heavy spending, and you may welcome a turn to a more frugal pace of living.

The frugal answer to personal consumption doesn't mean that you will become a tightwad. Far from that, you will probably find yourself wanting to buy higher quality merchandise, fewer items, and keep what you own in better repair. Being frugal means being careful and having an interest in quality. It doesn't mean that you stop spending.

One friend, a salesperson for a prestigious company, reduced his clothing costs while he upgraded the quality of his wardrobe. He decided to own only two suits. Both suits were solid colors, were hand tailored by Brooks Brothers, and were made from the most costly woolens. He had a variety of shirts and ties, and thus he never appeared to look the same. He was always regarded as being well dressed, and his clothing expense averaged less than $300 per year, which is a fraction of what most people in his position typically spend for clothes.

Being frugal with your consumption expenses lowers the break-even point of your budget. That gives you greater flexibility in organizing your life. It allows you to place your development as the first priority. It frees you from feeling trapped by the past image you have built up. That feeling about yourself is important now. It allows you to consider changes in the way you live without making a major break with your past before you may be ready for a change. It gives you a taste of freedom, but doesn't demand a major commitment.

If you have a family and you explain what you are trying to do, you should expect their support. Most families would be supportive, if they understand the purpose of a program to lower consumption spending. Children become more careful with their clothes, and teenagers often take a new pride in finding a part-time job. There is usually a sense of mutual helpfulness which all the money in the world can't buy.

Spend Money for New Insights

The development of skills usually involves the expenditure of money. You have prepared for these expenses by controlling your consumption spending. Now you should be ready to use these funds to their best advantage.

If you work for a corporation, this period will give you the incentive to enlarge your horizon about yourself as well as the company you work for. If you do not expand your scope of interests, you run the risk of becoming a disposable executive in the next stage of your life cycle. Without the infusion of insight of who you are, and what your corporation really is doing, you may appear stale to your superiors. In today's corporate world, if you appear stale in your fifties, you could be a prime candidate for forced early retirement.

If you are an entrepreneur or independent professional, now is the time to develop your business into new areas or start an additional business. Some businesspeople use this period to develop standards for their business and franchise their operations. Some persons leave the corporate world to begin business for themselves during this period. Their interests may have expanded beyond the scope that their corporation would allow, and they forsake the apparent security of a corporate job for work that is more closely tailored to their skills.

Prepare a Five-Year Life Plan

A life plan is similar to a career plan, except that a life plan includes a plan for your personal life as well as your career. This plan should be a simple statement of what you expect to be doing in all major areas of your life five years into the future. It should include a simple statement of your goals, training that you need, changes in your home location, financial and other key steps that will be necessary to accomplish that goal, and the results that you hope to achieve. These accomplishments need to be quite specific if the plan is to have value. The ideal complete plan should be one page in length, never more than two pages. The plan must be brief and to the point if it is to be effective.

During the midlife period of your life cycle, a life plan provides organization to offset the splintering effect of your emerging interests. In the preceding and following periods of your life cycle a formal plan would not be particularly useful. During those periods there is considerable stability in your thinking, and a plan is not really needed to help you clarify your direction.

The simple statement of the activities you expect to undertake will probably surprise you. The management of your time is now essential, and even with good time management, you will probably feel that you are under stress to accomplish more than ever before. Even placid people feel a considerable amount of stress during this period of the life cycle, and high-pressured people often comment that they feel overwhelmed. There is nothing wrong with stress at this period. In fact, it is an important source of energy, and it enables you to get things done. But stress sometimes takes its toll on health. Your life plan should include time for sports, running, or some physical effort that will act as a safety valve.

After you prepare your life plan, you should seek an objective review. A doctor, lawyer, investment counselor, accountant or career counselor is often a good choice for a reviewer. A close friend who has an eye for being candid and objective could also be a good choice. Sometimes workshops are available for this purpose. A review of your life plan should help you determine whether it is realistic. Most five-year life plans prepared by persons in their midlife period include major new efforts and commitments. They may reflect realistic capabilities, or they may simply be dreams. You need to have an independent opinion to test that you are on the right track.

Look at the Tax Consequences of Your Life Plan

The financial consequences of success are sharply higher taxes. As has been noted, the fruits of success are taxed unevenly with the system of progressive taxation. Those two facts are seldom considered by most persons in earlier stages of their life cycle. Most persons are then too much wrapped up in their work to give attention to the tax implications of their future success. During the midlife stage, simply to achieve self-fulfillment can be considered to be reward enough. Nevertheless, during the next stage of the life cycle, the maturity stage, the tax implications of the midlife efforts will become critically important. Now is the time to look ahead to that situation and keep an eye on the tax implications of your life plan.

KEY INCOME AND EXPENSE CATEGORIES

Income Taxes

If your life plan calls for you to increase your income substantially as an employee in a high-tax area, such as London, Boston, or New York, you should see what your after-tax income will amount to. If you would keep less than one-half of your pre-tax income, you should reconsider your plan. Nobody on a long-term basis should plan to turn over the greater portion of his or her additional efforts to the government. If you search, you will find a way in which your personal achievement and government tax policy can combine to permit you, rather than the government, to be the principal benefactor of your work.

You should look carefully at your expenses and at your work. For example, some couples have family incremental tax brackets of 70 percent and pay a cleaning lady $8.00 per hour. Those people would have to earn over $25 per hour pretax to break even paying their cleaning ladies. One solution would be to move to a small, modern apartment, where cleaning would not be a major problem. Another solution which is becoming more widespread is for the husband to reduce his workload, and spend more time helping with household chores.

Another solution would be to look for a way to barter services, or to join a barter club that provides a broadly based collection of goods and services. Usually barter clubs recommend that participants value their exchange at 50 percent of the retail price, which cuts the tax rate in half. Since compliance with reporting barter transactions is entirely voluntary, it is no secret that the Internal Revenue Service does not like them. Before you join one of these clubs, check carefully the way the club expects to protect its membership list. But in an area of rising tax rates, barter systems could become widespread.

Another tax issue is to choose a location for work that has a low tax rate. In some instances there are only a limited number of locations that would accommodate certain specialized work. For example, a New York neurosurgeon would not find similar work in a small mountain village. But these extremes are unusual. Most people can find work in the lower tax area. Some friends have taken major steps in this direction by working in overseas low tax areas. A friend who is an economist in Hong Kong earns three times as much on an after-tax basis as she would in London. And Hong Kong is now one of the most beautiful and civilized cities in the world.

An important tax issue is whether you would consider organizing your work as an independent businessperson, rather than as an employee. As an independent businessperson, you are entitled to all of the benefits and tax deductions of a self-employed person, and you are able to control your pension fund. Some companies now permit selected persons to work for them on an ongoing contractual basis. With this arrangement, you pay taxes as an independent businessperson. Most of these people offer unusual technical skills and need to show income from more than one source to qualify for this tax status. This arrangement would not bar you from a top position. Two friends are now chief executives of major companies after taking this route in their careers.

Most people are shocked at the tax implications of their life plan. It is a sad comment on the liberal ideals of most modern governments that the tax laws, if they would be guides to our work behavior, encourage the most talented and ambitious people to work steadily less as they become more widely recognized for their skills. But that is exactly what the tax laws are telling you to do. The government, of course, hopes that you will not be so rational, and that you will forge ahead, oblivious to the tax consequences of your efforts.

Despite the challenge of taxes, you don't live behind the Iron Curtain. You can do something about taxes. What you decide to do may involve changes or some inconvenience from a life plan that did not consider them. But you do have choices. The tax challenge is the most important financial issue you will likely face during your next 20 years. I have yet to hear of an instance in which a good solution couldn't be found.

Education

This is a time for you to learn more about your interests. This effort will require time and money, and at this stage of your life cycle, time is money.

Nevertheless, whenever you must choose between time for your education and greater income, you should invariably pursue education and forego the alternative of added income. This is a stage of your life cycle when you would receive more value from your added hours of education than you would benefit from added income. This is a time to rethink your directions. The insight that you obtain to make the right choices is critical.

Moreover, you will find any additional income will be taxed at an increasingly heavy rate, leaving you a relatively small amount of money to pocket. Your spending for education and training, however, may be tax-free. If the training is construed to be necessary for you to maintain your present work, it would represent a tax-deductible expense from your income and thus be paid with less costly tax-free dollars.

In the past decade there has been a major expansion of educational opportunities that are available throughout the

United States which fit the needs of people in the midlife stage of their life cycle. Community colleges, extension courses of major universities, trade schools, lectures, cultural shows, group reading programs, book series, performances, auditions, tours, new magazines and a proliferation of organizations for a wide variety of interests from sky diving to china painting have grown rapidly. There is now virtually no activity or interest that does not have instruction offered by an educational institution, publication, newsletter, or association. One of the most interesting new directions in this widening scope of education is the growth of alternative universities. These educational institutions offer degrees for studies in areas in which the traditional universities do not have programs. Never before has so much educational variety been so available to so many people.

One friend was a carpenter, and in his early forties found his interests carried him into cabinetry more than construction. He studied cabinetry, worked during his off hours for a cabinet maker, but found this work lacked fulfillment for him. This person enjoyed working with people, and the traditional work of carpentry and cabinetry was more production oriented than people oriented. He began to work as a home alteration specialist, using his skill in woodworking and his enjoyment in working with people. He was able to communicate well with his customers in a business that is not known for good communication and began one of the most successful businesses in his area.

This case illustrates the importance of using education as a driving wedge to further your development during the midlife stage. The first effort that you take to broaden your interests will not always be in the direction of your final interests. Part of the benefit of taking new directions is finding what suits best as well as what suits least. The latter is just as important as the former to give you the focus you will need as this period draws to a close.

This educational experience is your only sure antidote to feeling trapped in your mode of living and working. Unless you have such a safety valve, your feelings of being caught in life's vise may cripple your spirit, and you may mistakenly narrow your outlook almost out of spite or dejection. The frustrations of the midlife period create an enormous amount of tension and resentment. Your exploration of yourself through the pursuit of new areas of interest will keep your spirits buoyant and give you a way to wipe away the blues you will surely feel in this stage. Once a glimmer of hope shines through even a crack in the darkness, your energies will be applied in a constructive manner. During the midlife stage of the life cycle, that is half of the battle.

Secondary Occupation

Your job may be a source of particular concern to you during this period, especially if you are an employee. You may find that the reputation you built up during your adulthood stage is not enough to satisfy you. Your new interests and new directions carry you far beyond your past interests. However, your employer may continue to evaluate you on the basis of your past momentum. Thus you and your employer are looking past each other.

At the same time, you come to grips with the organizational pyramid of the company or government you work for. The organizational pyramid means that in any organization there are only a very few senior positions, and the larger the size of the organization, the greater will be the likelihood that you will not be chosen to fill a top position. During the adulthood stage, most persons believe that they could storm the ramparts of the senior positions of any organization and, through their hard work, win the grateful approval of management. The midlife period brings an important shift in thinking. Such easy success no longer seems assured. Moreover, success is not measured so obviously in this stage. Your horizon of thought is expanding, and earlier measures of accomplishment may now seem shallow and inadequate.

This situation has largely pertained to men until recently. But increasingly the situation also applies to women. In fact, if the trend toward increasing participation of women in the work force is carried forward in the coming decade, an ever-larger number of women will face exactly the same situation.

The solutions many people make are either to remain with their organization and hope for the best or to send out resumes and hope that another firm will offer them a better position. In a few cases these approaches work, but only if the positions provide new challenges that correspond to the person's emerging interests. Often the new positions provide more money but not career satisfaction. I have found that most people in this stage of the life cycle trade one inadequate job for another. The only consistent exceptions are people who become company presidents. These people invariably enjoy their work more than people who have lesser positions.

There are very few presidential positions among the large companies. But there are many top positions in small companies. This fact is perhaps the single most important point about careers in the midlife stage of the life cycle. Some of the most successful developments in careers include persons who have reached a high level of competence and built up capital during their adulthood stage. These persons also maintained an avocation or a secondary occupation that provided them with a personal and independent business view. During the latter part of their midlife stage, they used their capital to open their own business.

One friend had spent 20 years working for two truck manufacturers, first as a design engineer and subsequently as section head for production. He often thought about buying a dealership during those years. I accompanied him when he called on a friend whose father owned a small dealership that was for sale, and we discussed many other potential purchases over the years. In each case this person was testing his skills and gaining knowledge about the truck dealership business.

Despite his work experience, the essential ingredient to his eventual purchase of a dealership was his avocation in restoring old Packard cars. His passion for these cars was unbounded. At one time he owned six, all in various stages of repair, which he stored in rented garages. He knew many people who also collected these cars throughout the country, and he bought and sold dozens of the cars. Through this avocation of buying, restoring, and selling Packards, he developed sales and marketing skills. These skills had not been developed by his full-time job. His avocation rounded his business experience and gave him the broad competence in sales and marketing he needed when he and a partner eventually purchased one of the largest dealerships in the nation.

There is a basic reason why you need to develop an avocation during the midlife stage. During the period up to this stage, your avocation may reflect your vocational interests more truly than your job. Your regular work usually reflects the decisions you made as a younger person, when your parents and teachers influenced your vocational decision. Your avocation is an activity you alone decide to pursue. It is usually not essential for this activity to provide you with money, but it is essential that it provides you with enjoyment. Your avocation allows you to perfect your emerging personal interests in a semi-commercial way, and it provides you with an alternative to your regular job at a time when you may need alternatives.

Most avocations or secondary occupations would lose money if they were placed on a business basis. There is nothing wrong with this. Avocations usually need seed money to begin and subsidies to keep them going for a few years before some of these can turn profitable. You should arrange your budget to provide for an avocation, and you should nourish this important interest.

Entertainment

During this stage of your life cycle you should give special attention to keep in close touch with your friends and loved ones. You have a tendency to lose contact with people as your interests become inner directed. Your thinking may even become self-centered, and friendships seldom flourish with that attitude of the mind.

There is nothing wrong with the emphasis on inner direction of this period in your life cycle, but it should be kept within bounds. Ironically, you need your friends now more than ever before. They provide a way of enabling you to keep your balance. They remind you of the importance of humanity in your life, no matter how frustrated you may become with your work or discouraged with your accomplishments.

You should plan to spend at least two occasions each week with your friends, and if you have a family, you should get together with other families. Some persons prefer entertainment that centers around sports events, and others enjoy direct participation in sports such as tennis, running, or golf. These activities may seem like an enormous amount of entertaining or association to many persons in their midlife period. You should encourage activities that bring friends and you together, even if the effort seems to be more trouble than it is worth.

If you have a family, you should set up a kid's day once each month. During this day, put your children in charge, and let them choose how you spend your day. Let them decide where you might travel or what sport you might play. This can open channels of communication between you and your children, and also take your mind off yourself.

None of these activities needs to cost much money. You can play tennis in most areas at municipal courts, and running with a friend requires only a pair of good shoes. Getting together with friends doesn't involve much cost. Whatever these costs might be, you should not be so self-centered now that you feel that you cannot afford it. Be prepared to pay this expense, and from time to time, even go beyond what you think is appropriate.

If you lose contact with your friends or your family, your financial consequences will be much greater than the costs of keeping up your friendships. If your inner-directed concern takes your attention away from your family, you may lose your family. One friend became so wrapped up in his work that he and his wife were divorced. He subsequently married a woman who, in many ways, resembled his first wife. One time, at what appeared to be the right moment, I remarked how similar his two wives appeared to be. This friend agreed, and recalled that he lost his first wife because he had allowed himself to become a victim of his worry about himself. His sense of personal failure had run so deeply that he felt alienated by his wife and family, and he left them. He later realized that he had loved and really needed his wife, as well as his three children. But by that time it was too late to change the events of the past. He had lacked a bridge to get him across a temporary sense of failure.

Many divorces in the midlife stage reflect the effects of a temporary period of misgiving and soul searching. Some divorces are probably unnecessary, if a way could be found to get through the midlife period with more support, possibly from close friends or counseling.

The financial implications of divorce are almost always difficult. Your capital is split, and your borrowing capacity is usually reduced. You may be required to sell assets at a time when markets may not be favorable. Moreover, during a divorce, your business and financial judgment is not as sharp as it otherwise would be. These costs can amount to a large loss.

Nevertheless, some divorces are beneficial. Some persons marry and then mutually develop into different and incompatible ways of living. The midlife challenge puts your development and the development of your spouse under the glare of scrutiny. You are challenged to see whether your spouse is right for you, and whether your past way of living is right for you. If it is not right, then this period is a time when you may make a change. When the change is beneficial, all parties develop better than if they lived in a state of siege or in an uncaring situation.

With a few persons the concern over personal problems in the midlife stage becomes so overwhelming that they take their own life. This loss is irreparable, and I believe, in every case it is unnecessary. One college friend was at the top of his class and could provide solutions to problems in mathematics and physics when nobody else would know how to begin to solve the problems. I was shocked to learn one day that he had taken his life and that during the year preceding that event he had felt plagued with a sense of personal failure. He had needed a bridge to get him across what was really a temporary problem, and unfortunately he had none.

Our friends and loved ones are a bridge to help us across our troubles during the midlife stage of our life cycle. There is no other safe bridge when the chips are down. A small amount of expense and a large amount of thought about our friends and loved ones usually represent money and time well spent. Moreover, generosity on our part at this time reaps enormous dividends and is insurance that we will make the right decisions with our lives. Our concern for our friends and loved ones is reflected back to us. The midlife stage is a period when we need this reflection to see ourselves as we really are and to give us the strength that we need to cope with this period.

KEY ASSETS AND LIABILITIES

Debt Securities

During the midlife stage of your life cycle you should give emphasis to investments that provide liquidity. Short-term debt securities should be the primary focus for your savings. You should become familiar with the wide variety of securities in this investment category, but there are three categories of short-term debt investments that you should give particular attention to.

The first category is U.S. Treasury bills. These securities are the safest and most liquid security in existence. They are backed by the full faith and guarantee of the United States government. They are even technically one notch ahead of all other U.S. Treasury obligations, since they are a current bill of exchange for dollars rather than a promise to pay dollars sometime in the future. The distinction would be important only in the improbable situation of a moratorium on repayment of United States government obligations. Under those unlikely conditions, Treasury bills would continue to be liquid, because they would be considered an exchange and not covered by a disruption of the promise for repayment. The point is important only in emphasizing the premier position that Treasury bills hold among debt investments.

The difficulty of Treasury bills is that they are issued by the Federal Reserve, which acts as agent for the U.S. Treasury, in a minimal amount of $10,000. Larger amounts may be purchased in increments of $5,000, such as $15,000, $20,000, and so forth. Nevertheless, the minimal amount is beyond the reach of many small and some medium-sized investors.

A second group of short-term debt securities is offered by most banks, as well as many other financial institutions. These are term savings deposits or a similar type of debt instrument by nonbank financial institutions. These deposits have an advantage of being available in small minimal amounts. Often the minimal amount is $100. The relatively small denomination of these deposits and large number of issuing financial institutions makes them easy to obtain. Moreover, because they are deposits, they are at the top of the liabilities of a financial institution's balance sheet. That position indicates that they are first to be paid in the event of the failure of the institution. In addition, federally chartered financial institutions and others with federal agency membership have insurance that guarantees repayment in each name up to $100,000.

The disadvantages of these smaller-sized deposits is that they are not both liquid and high yielding. When they are liquid, their yields are relatively low. If you purchase a six-month deposit, you receive a lower rate of interest than you would receive for a five-year deposit. The five-year deposit cannot be sold back to the financial institution except at a major penalty of interest. During this stage of your life cycle you should choose liquidity and accept the lower rate of interest. You need financial flexibility most of all at this time, and liquidity gives you that flexibility.

For large investors, most banks sell negotiable certificates of deposit. These certificates of deposit may be sold in the open market at any time to other banks and larger securities houses. They pay somewhat higher yields than Treasury bills and are also at the top of the liabilities of the financial institution. They are covered by government-sponsored insurance programs up to $100,000 of the face value of the certificate. Their principal disadvantage for most people is the large amount that is required for minimal purchase.

The third type of short-term investment is the short-term money-market mutual fund. This type of mutual fund owns Treasury bills, negotiable certificates of deposit, and sometimes commercial paper from corporations, and it sells shares of this combined pool of funds to the public. The money-market mutual funds buy high-yielding short-term securities and make them available to small investors. These funds are a recent development, and their assets have increased enormously over the past few years. They provide a solution to the problem of combining liquidity and high yield.

Money-market funds involve two risks that are relatively insignificant at present but should be considered before you invest in them. The first risk is the money-market fund itself. The management of these funds stands between you and the institutions that have issued their promise to pay you. If a fund management should be remiss or become involved with irregularities that reduce the value of its assets, you could suffer.

You should check the reputation of any fund you invest in. Many funds are associated with major or highly regarded financial houses, and your judgment of the parent may serve as a proxy for the management of the fund. Even so, you may wish to look into the background of the principals of the fund. As a start, review the biographical information provided by a fund in its prospectus. You may wish to make inquiries concerning past associations of the principals. Reputation is important, since these funds are one of the least regulated parts of the financial services industry, and past habits of principals may be an important guide to their future behavior.

The second issue of money-market funds is whether they have purchased quality assets. Financial markets do not distinguish closely between the quality of most financial institutions, largely because investors believe that short-term paper of financial institutions is virtually risk-free. Most investors believe that there is an implied assurance from regulatory agencies that bank failures will not occur. This conventional wisdom suggests that there may be bank mergers but not bank failures, and holders of certificates of deposit would not be affected by mergers. Still, it never hurts to be cautious when you are investing in deposits and debt instruments. There appears to be a wide range in the quality of the banks that money-market funds include, and it does not appear to involve a sacrifice in yield to select a fund with certificates of deposit of high quality banks.

One way to review the quality of banks and corporations in money-market funds is to check their ratings in Moody's and Standard & Poor's. Use the debt rating of these services rather than commercial paper ratings, since debt ratings tend to be more discriminating. Most public libraries, brokerage houses, and bank libraries have these debt-rating reports.

Bank Loan

A line of credit, which represents an unused bank loan, is a major financial tool you should develop, even if you never use it. Lines of credit do not involve points or fixed-payment periods, as do second mortgages or installment loans. They also do not require stated purposes, as do all other personal loans. A line of credit is a more flexible way of borrowing large amounts of money than virtually any other method. It is often the least expensive way you can borrow large amounts.

Some banks do not offer lines of credit to individuals, so you may have to shop around to find a bank that offers this service. You should begin with the bank that handles your mortgage or checking or savings account. See your local branch manager, ask this person if the bank offers a personal line of credit, and inquire what the upper limit is. Banks often give special names to this type of loan commitment, but most bankers will immediately recognize what you have in mind.

A personal line of credit is an open-ended loan commitment on the part of a bank to lend you money up to a prearranged maximum amount. This type of personal loan commitment is identical to loan commitments made to large corporations and government agencies. The bank's credit department reviews your assets and your reputation of paying bills, and makes a decision of whether you are creditworthy. The bank only has your reputation to guide it, just as it is guided by a corporation's ability to show profits or a government agency to continue to collect revenues. Without confidence in your character, the bank would have little to justify its loan.

The emphasis placed on your pattern of regular debt payments you built during your adulthood stage of the life cycle now begins to pay dividends. In considering a loan commitment application, a bank's credit department reviews whether your past record shows that you paid your debts regularly and promptly. If you have a perfect or a near-perfect record, they will probably conclude that you have the characteristics of financial integrity. If you have avoided a police record and show other indications of stability, they will probably further conclude that you are a person who has character. All of this may sound quaint, even corny. It is actually a very serious conclusion. That conclusion can open the door to money which could enable you to do something with your life that might otherwise be denied you.

You should ask for the upper limit that the bank permits for this type of loan commitment. This loan commitment does not cost you a penny until you use it. For this reason alone it is probably the biggest bargain in financial services available to you. In contrast, most corporate and some government agency borrowers pay a commitment fee from .25 percent to 1.25 percent for the privilege of having this kind of open-ended loan. Banks have not recognized that they could quite easily charge a comparable commitment fee to individuals, and these customers would still receive fair value for such a commitment. Of course, their oversight is your gain.

Some smaller banks do not have a formal personal loan commitment program, but they make the service available to their well-known customers. You would need to know your branch manager personally before you would qualify for this loan commitment. Say hello to this person when you are in the bank, and send a Christmas card.

Large banks usually have programs that are centrally administered, and you can make an inquiry about personal loans at any branch. Be sure to ask about the program in a special visit for this purpose, and call ahead to set up an appointment. This is a formal way of conducting yourself, and bankers usually like appointments, since they tend to indicate that you have given some thought to the matter you wish to discuss. An appointment suggests that you have not stopped by to see them on the spur of the moment.

If a banker turns you down, don't get discouraged. It's always a bit of a blow when you are turned down for any credit request, and a low feeling at that time is perfectly normal. Keep your spirits bright, but whatever you do, don't try to forget about the rejection. If you are sent a negative notice, you should ask to talk with the branch manager again. In this conversation, ask the manager exactly what weakness in your application was responsible for the bank's response. Be sure to ask this person to be specific, and take notes of his or her comments. If the branch manager appears a bit vague, it means he or she doesn't have all of the facts from the credit department. Then, in a respectful and clear voice, ask if the manager could obtain this information from the bank's credit department, and set up another meeting.

Your objective should be to discover exactly what you must do to raise your credit rating to an acceptable level. You will then follow these points to the letter, and after you have fulfilled the requirements, you will apply for a loan commitment again. You will also tell your branch manager that you intend to do these things and ask him or her to be sure to retain your file. This is an important step, because you will then have received an implied commitment on the part of that branch manager to give you recognition for your future accomplishments. Maintaining your file is important, because branch managers are often transferred to other locations, and your file should be ready for the new branch manager to review.

Housing

The midlife stage of your life cycle is not the time to buy a larger home. The purchase of a larger house involves further leverage, and the midlife stage is a period when you should reduce your leverage and build up your liquidity. You should keep your leverage as low as possible during this period, because low leverage reduces your financial risk and increases your ability to manage your life in a flexible manner. You can make changes in your life more easily if your leverage is low. In fact, it may be a worthwhile goal to eliminate your leverage completely.

In recent years this recommendation has not been widely practiced. Real estate is one major investment that is widely held and that has been able to outpace inflation. The only other investments that have rivaled housing in investment appreciation in recent years have been gold, silver, and precious gems. Moreover, homes represent the only investment of most people that provides tax advantages through deductions for local taxes and interest expense.

There is a strong attraction to continue making investments in real estate by persons in this stage of their life cycle, either through direct acquisition or through participations in limited partnerships or shares. It is possible that real estate will continue to show a continued rise during the coming decade, although, as was discussed earlier, that outlook is not entirely clear.

Nevertheless, in your midlife stage, the outlook for real estate really doesn't matter. Illiquid, highly leveraged investments, such as real estate, aren't the type of new investment that should be made by persons in this stage of their life cycle. The time for real estate investment was during the adulthood stage, and real estate will again be an investment vehicle during the subsequent maturity stage of the life cycle.

This is the time to consider the borrowing ability you may have on the real estate you already have purchased. You should discuss this borrowing potential with a bank or savings and loan officer, simply to obtain a general idea of what the borrowing potential might amount to. You should be prepared to use the financial potential that you have built up. You may need the money to start a new business, further an educational program to develop skills, or even to finance what used to be called a pilgrimage and now is sometimes called a regenerative vacation.

You should shop for the best terms. You should use as much care in this shopping as you did when you bought the real estate in the first place. For many people, real estate equity represents their single, largest source of funds. Securing the best terms for these funds will make a major difference in your balance sheet during your next stage of the life cycle.

Your first step is to draw up a short list of potential lenders. This list should include, at the top, the financial institution that may already hold your first mortgage, if it remains unpaid. You should discuss your borrowing plans with this institution, because it is closely familiar with your credit rating. Moreover, this institution will probably want to keep you as a customer, and may be expected to give you favorable terms.

You should also contact at least two other potential lenders, including savings and loan associations, banks, or mortgage brokers with whom you have had some past business relationship. If you don't have past relationships, look for lenders that are located in the immediate neighborhood of the real estate that you wish to borrow against. These lenders should be familiar with the property, and their proximity to your property gives you an understandable business reason for calling on them.

The terms of your request should include two important considerations. First, you should compare interest rates on a fully adjusted basis. That means you should add the cost of loan applications, legal fees, and points to the total interest cost. Points are front-end fees that are charged separately from the interest expense of the loan. Lenders often like to consider them separately so that they get cash quickly and hope that you may overlook this cost in making competitive comparisons. If you have difficulty making this calculation, ask the lender to do it. If this person brushes the request aside, don't worry. Leave the meeting and then call the controller's department of the lending institution, tell them of your interest in a loan and your wish to have a fully complete interest rate charge. This is the department with persons who are technically equipped to answer your question accurately. They should help you quickly, often while you are on the phone.

Family

Throughout history, family ties have always been a key source of funds. In fact, during most of the past millennium, the family has been the principal source of funds for most people. That tradition continues today in large parts of the world, including areas in Africa, Asia, and Latin America that are largely noncommercial, and do not have a widespread availability of financial institutions. It is also the principal source of funds for people in most Communist countries, particularly for purposes that do not further the official interests of the governments in those countries.

The extended family is a type of financial institution. The old members of a family accumulate assets which they lend, give, or bequest to younger members who need capital for homes, youngsters, or a career.

Family members who lend to persons in their midlife stage are usually considerably older. These persons understand the yearnings of the midlife stage and, unlike members of a family that are younger, have both the personal understanding and often the financial resources to be of help. They represent important sources of financing that are often overlooked in today's highly commercial world.

Perhaps we have become so commercial that we have put blinders on our thinking and blocked out the extended family. Our greater mobility has scattered families all over the United States, and in some cases, all over the world. Communication and the sharing of personal hopes and needs has become less meaningful. Many members of a family wouldn't recognize other members if they passed each other on the street.

Years ago members of several branches of my family would get together for family picnics on the Fourth of July at a particular uncle's farm in Ohio. A professional photographer would arrive between the time of the pot-luck supper and the cracking of the ice for home-made ice cream and take everybody's picture. The pictures show that about 60 people used to attend those functions. I recall that following discussions about politics, business was the most frequent topic of conversation among the men, and someone who wanted to expand a farm, launch a new business, or find a new job had a ready audience. I should add that the audience was not always entirely sympathetic, but it was an understanding and almost always a helpful audience.

Except in parts of the South and among immigrants from Mexico and parts of Asia, I have noticed that extended family meetings have diminished in importance. Yet the round-robin cassette may provide one way of keeping news of a family in circulation. This is a 90-minute cassette that is circulated in a prearranged mailing sequence, each person recording five or ten minutes of comments. The comments are based on what the person hears from earlier parts of the tape, as well as comments about the local family. The round-robin family tape can give a more vital feeling of family closeness than letters or relatively brief long distance telephone calls.

Most families include one or more persons who have accumulated sizeable amounts of assets and who are in a position to invest part of these assets. These persons will want a fair return on their money. They may want a portion of the equity of your activities, although these requests are unusual. Family members regard their feelings as an important part of transactions, and to the extent that these feelings gain you a sympathetic audience, you should benefit from them. But your business proposal must stand on its own financial feet, and you should prepare your proposal to a relative with as much care as you would use in making the proposal to your banker.

Once an agreement is reached, it should be placed in writing and signed by you, your spouse, and your relative. If the relative has a spouse, both persons should sign. You don't want your relative to change his or her mind a year after you reach an agreement, because of an unexpected dislike to something you or your spouse might say. The quick communication of a family works both ways. It opens doors as well as closes doors. To be sure that you will not have future difficulties with your source of funds, put your agreement in writing.

Friends

In addition to your family, your friends could be an important source of funds. Most people in their midlife stage have made contact with a wide circle of friends. Teachers, church friends, families of children who associate with your children, clubs, colleagues in professional or fraternal associations, working associates, bank and other financial friends, classmates from high school or college, insurance agents, tax and accounting friends, proprietors of all kinds of businesses from auto repair shops to dry cleaners form your circle of friends and acquaintances. Some of those persons would qualify as lenders to you, but you don't know who they are. In fact, the experience of persons who have sought funds from friends suggests that a prospective borrower will probably omit the best prospects if they are qualified on the basis of general impressions.

This point was brought out clearly by a friend who had worked for a commercial credit company for many years and wanted to start his own business. He had saved virtually no money and found that he could not borrow more than three month's living expenses from his bank. That amount was not enough to provide capital for the business and provide food and shelter during the startup period of the new business.

Through his business contacts, this person had made the friendship of a wide number of persons, and these persons developed a respect for his good judgment in making credit decisions. One of these persons was the owner of a paper box manufacturing company, and during one of their conversations, commented that there was nobody doing a good job in recycling used paper boxes. He suggested that this person should start the business, and he let him use a corner of his plant without charge. The business grew rapidly, and five years later the used paper box dealer bought a warehouse as large as the paper box manufacturing plant.

I asked this person if he had an inkling that his customer would be such a helpful friend. He said that he had never dreamed that such an offer would be made, since the paper box manufacturer had a reputation of being a particularly ungenerous person. However, this manufacturer needed some-
· body to service the used paper box part of his business, and his business acumen, not his humanity, forced his generosity to reveal itself.

Many people, of course, do not receive opportunities of this type, or if they do, they do not feel that they wish to enter a new or different business. The change from credit investigation to used box collection is a major shift in business and is a broader jump than most people would feel comfortable in making. Yet everybody can develop the format of what they might wish to accomplish, and take steps to let their friends know of their plans.

The first step in letting friends know of your interest is simply to tell them, and ask them if they would like to look at a brief outline of your proposal. Then prepare about a three-page description of your proposal, and include an indication of the profit you would hope to earn and the money you would need. You should not ask friends on a hit-and-miss basis. Rather, you should draw up a list with at least 25 names and preferably 50 or more. You should always let your friends initiate a response to this proposal. If they are interested, they will respond. Don't worry if most friends never respond, since this is typical. Most friends don't like to tell you that they don't have much money, or they don't like your proposal for one reason or another, or that their wife or husband is upset. If you don't get a response, let the matter drop. If you do this, you won't lose a friend in the process.

One or more of your friends will likely respond favorably. You should ask this person or group to get together to review your plans in more detail. At this meeting you should have a list of your proposed customers and more detailed financial projections. You should explain that the meeting is for information purposes only and that you will not ask anybody for a financial commitment at the meeting. This point is important, because most persons are reluctant to pursue business opportunities with friends for fear that their personal association may be injured by the business proposals. To avoid this problem, at the end of the meeting ask anybody who would wish to pursue the business proposal further to contact you later.

You may get a call from one or more of these friends. If you do, discuss the proposal further, and then ask your friend what additional information is needed for an indication of a financial interest. By that time, your friend will have reached the level of interest that is great enough so that he or she will be expecting your request. Moreover, by this time, your friend may voluntarily indicate a financial interest, which would be best of all.

It is also possible that nobody will call you. If you have no other possible sources of financing, don't be discouraged. Let this business proposal drop. Put it away. You still have your friends. Moreover, some friends will keep the proposal in mind. Months later, or even a year or two later, conditions may change for a particular friend, and that person may call you and reawaken the proposal.

But don't wait for this to happen. Begin to think about your next business proposal. Study your ideas, and prepare another three-page summary. Prepare another list of friends, adding a few names to your old list, and follow the procedure again. I have seen this approach in operation many times, and eventually it works. Sometimes it takes three attempts and three business proposals before there is a meeting of minds and a business is formed. Friends try to do the right things in your behalf, and in one way or another, they always succeed in helping you.

Chapter 11

MATURITY AND PASSING THE TORCH: AGE 51 TO 65

*T*HE maturity stage is one of the most gratifying periods of the life cycle. It is a time where the torch of experience is passed to others, particularly younger persons. This is the age of teaching. It is a settled time, when all of the pieces of life seem to come together and make sense, and when conflicts occur, you are able to endure them more equitably than ever before.

The strength of this period lies in the ability to act as a teacher. This is the period that sometimes is coupled with the adulthood stage, when, as a helpful tutor, you can help a young man or woman in that earlier stage. The strongest persons of this stage of life are mentors who pass along their experience to the next generation, who in turn reshape and reuse this experience in their own way. The enjoyment of learning a trade or profession in the adulthood stage is now mirrored with an enjoyment of teaching and acting as a guide to learning. This is a time for renewal. I have found that people who most enjoyed learning a skill or trade in their earlier stage of the life cycle greatly enjoy the maturity stage. They instinctively understand that they now sit on the other side of the table and that a new social responsibility is now expected of them.

Passing the torch of experience involves a sharp shift in focus from the preceding period of midlife challenge. This shift takes you from being deeply self-conscious and concerned with the inner working of the mind to that of being an actor, and sometimes a bit of a show-off. The change is dramatic, and it sometimes happens quite rapidly.

During the maturity stage of the life cycle, a groundswell of confidence comes over you. The confidence reflects a new sense of acceptance of your weakness as well as your strengths. It is as if the fire of the midlife challenge has burned away whatever is not truly your personality, and only your most durable structure remains. Then in the maturity stage the fire recedes, and a sense of grateful abundance quickens the heart. You welcome the world.

People in the maturity stage of their life cycle don't worry about themselves the way that they did during the preceding stage. They are more outgoing and more concerned about others. In passing along their experience, they want to be sure that the recipient will be able to carry on. The maturity stage is one of caring in this sense. It is a period of sensitivity to other people's feelings and hopes, of seeing how these individual feelings can be nourished to support technical skills.

The concern for other people is perhaps the most obvious characteristic of the period. It is also the basis of strength which is essential for the striving of leadership that is part of this period. There is, in fact, a certain amount of self-sacrificing of one's personal goals during the period, so that others can develop. If there is any sense of urgency, it is to awaken in others their opportunities.

I have been impressed with the ways persons in the maturity stage of their life cycle accomplish this task. They invariably develop a unique sense of style, and the best develop a witty yet completely humane sense of humor. They often use a wink, a wry smile, a nod, or a gesture to show their good nature. Their humor conveys the message that a conflict need not harm but can be overcome, that everybody can benefit and possibly be better off as a result. The humor of this stage of the life cycle suggests that there is continuity to life, and that given the right kind of encouragement, people will weather whatever difficulties that may come along.

This is the period Plato talked about in the *Republic,* when philosopher kings should rule. That book recommends that persons who assume command of society should not rule before they had progressed through a rigorous training, corresponding to the earlier stages of the life cycle. Plato saw this period as one of leadership, the culmination of a lifetime of preparation in various types of technical skills. Plato stresses the point that leadership is not the same as technical expertise but is a different quality of mind and an empathetic feeling toward other persons.

Leadership is keenly felt by many people in this stage of the life cycle. One friend, who is a member of many fraternal organizations, remarked that men in their fifties join alumni organizations and run for school boards because they feel a strong compulsion to try their skills at leadership, and these organizations provide a quicker way of displaying this leadership than their regular work or other social activities.

The core of leadership, I believe, is a deep concern for the persons who are being led. Field Marshall Montgomery of the British Army, who first turned the tide of World War II against the Germans at El Alamein in North Africa, said that he was successful mainly because each member of his army believed that he would never send a man into battle unless there was a good chance that he could come out alive. As Montgomery retreated across North Africa, he conserved his manpower and conveyed to his troops that he was concerned most of all with their welfare. When the time came for his army to attack Rommel, Montgomery had devoted troops who were willing to follow what appeared to be an almost suicidal tank attack on the German forces. Montgomery had recently received major armored weapons and tank reinforcements from the United States, but he did not show these superior reinforcements to his troops to ensure the surprise to the Germans. The results were exactly as Montgomery had hoped for, and the British Army attacked successfully.

The example of General Montgomery represents an extreme situation, but I have found frequent similar situations in business and government. Often, in large organizations, a department chief wants to make a name for himself or herself and expects the members of the department to produce Herculean results, which the department chief will use at a presentation. It doesn't take many weeks of night work, sudden changes in schedules, and emergency calls on weekends to convince the deparment's workers that something is wrong. They quicky sense that they are being exploited by a leader who has little concern with their welfare, but rather skims the cream from their work and sets them out again on other projects. Most of life involves the skimming of the best of our efforts, but where we work for somebody who has the quality of leadership, we don't feel exploited.

The leader always gives back as much as the worker provides. The return to the worker is always in the form of a personal recognition and a reward that is appropriate for the work. A leader provides a sense of fairness that gives him or her control of the workers. Without this sense of fairness and personal recognition, workers will be indifferent or abandon a leader, if they possibly can do so.

Not everybody, of course, fully masters the challenge of this stage of the life cycle. In business, that mastery occurs when a person manages a company. That position requires the greatest amount of leadership, the greatest commitment to people, and is the most difficult position of any to fill. It makes no difference how small or large the company may be. The issue of leadership is the same.

Almost always, full leadershp requires a major shift in emphasis and a shift in the focus of a career. The persons who have developed competence in their adulthood stage and developed their inner identity during midlife now suddenly shift their focus, and their interests broaden. They no longer search deeper into their specialized fields, but take on broad tasks of managing the welfare of people.

I wonder whether there is any formal training for leadership that is fully effective. I have observed, however, that in almost every instance in which a person became president or manager of a company, he or she had enjoyed meaningful friendships earlier and often a good marriage. The stories about sacrificing one's family and friends to become president don't often hold up in practice, and I have found them to be rare. Few people will entrust their business well-being to somebody who doesn't have their welfare at heart.

There are, of course, many persons who rise to high rank in a business or profession but never hold a major position of leadership. Often these persons earn large amounts of money and enjoy positions of high respect. Most are competent, and some are exceptionally talented. Yet there is a difference between them and the manager of a company.

I have found that there is a simple test to determine whether someone you meet has the potential to lead a company. I usually judge correctly after I have met someone and ask myself two questions. The first question is whether this person looks at me squarely and talks with me in a clear voice. The second question is whether the person understands my point of view and treats this view objectively. Within a few minutes of conversation, if I have not been made aware of the person's business position, I will often make a mental note of what I think his or her position might be. In most cases, when I answer yes to both questions and the person is in the maturity stage of the life cycle, the person is the president of a company or a leader in a profession.

A more common response of persons in their maturity stage is to believe that they should accept the limitations of their situation. They believe that they are doing the best they can as a highly paid employee. The price that these people pay is considerable. They willingly corral the expression of their style of leadership.

All organizations require a willingness of employees to defer to the head of the company. This willingness to endorse and accept another person's style and direction of leadership is necessary if an organization is to function successfully. From an organizational point of view, hard-working, insightful, cooperative, and self-limiting employees are essential to the company's success. But the business requirements of a corporation, union, or government department are quite different from the personal need to show leadership of individuals in their maturity stage of the life cycle.

My first job was a junior member of the economics department of the Federal Reserve Bank, and I reported to a person who was in the maturity stage of his life cycle. This person was a superb teacher. In fact, virtually all the practical technical skills I have used regularly in the past 20 years are due to what I learned from this person and a high school mathematics teacher. I am not sure that I was the best of the lot in my department, since I never completely accepted the Federal Reserve System's economic dogma of the time. For example, in those days inflation was not supposed to be due to the heavy hands at the government printing presses, but was supposed to be due to a somewhat vague economic concept of residuals of the public's liquidity preferences. Nevertheless, I dutifully performed my job and learned to organize vast amounts of data and other information. This person was, if ever I can use the word appropriately, a genius at this task. He could take a mountain of paper, memo notes, and smudged charts and find the thread that would weave them together.

As I worked with this person, I increasingly felt a sense of incompleteness to his life. He had reached a respectable level in the Federal Reserve hierarchy, but there always was reticence whenever he would be drawn to conclusions that led him beyond what he considered to be acceptable by the Board of Governors. That organization is a low-key but effective censor of all activities of the Federal Reserve System. It was as if his mind worked beautifully until he came to a glass wall. Then, for no reason that I could understand at the time, he would suddenly stop. He would either abandon his conclusions or find some way of covering the material without coming to a conclusion.

On several of these occasions, I asked him why he would not follow through with what I felt were his conclusions, and he would answer obliquely, saying that Federal Reserve policy would prefer a different approach. The real reason, I believe, was his belief that he had no alternative to his work at the bank, and he feared censure or even expulsion from the bank if he should try to present his personal convictions. During a trip, waiting at a bar in an airport, he told me that he had been a social activist in the South during the early 1930s, years before this movement achieved its current political support. This activity, which reflected his deeply felt sense of equality and fairness for all people, had been disclosed after World War II in an unfavorable light. He believed that this disclosure was the cause of his being fired, of all places, from a government job just as his wife had delivered their first daughter. The shock was traumatic, and he resolved that he would not fight the system again.

I believe that this story has been repeated thousands of times, perhaps millions of times. The details would change, but the theme is the same. In the course of most people's lives there are major periods of stress, where their own individuality runs counter to the interests of a company, institution, or government agency. The institution acts in a way to ensure conformity and long-range continuity. The censure, so far as the individual is concerned, can often appear as punishment. When this happens and the cost of personal fulfillment appears to be too great, the person gives up an important part of his or her personal development. Mastering the maturity stage of the life cycle, then, appears wonderful as an idea, but one too risky to put into practice. These people tell themselves that they are acting in a reasonable or practical manner. Almost with a welcoming sigh of relief, they voluntarily put blinders on themselves so that they do not stray from their regular path.

There are two individuals who come to mind when I think of persons who have succeeded in mastering the maturity stage of their life cycle. Each moved in quite different types of business circles. One is a millionaire, the other is a person of more modest means. Each took a different path, but both shared the same basic approach to themselves, the people around them, and their work.

The first person is chairman of an international corporation that involves resources in all five continents and has a major involvement of the United States and other governments in its activities. It would be difficult to find a corporation that required a broader perspective or required the reconciling of a wider variety of conflicting views. This corporation was at one time a part of a conglomerate corporation, but it was subsequently divested, because this person convinced the head of the conglomerate that the benefits of divestiture would outweigh continuing operation as a subsidiary. This subsidiary had become one of the conglomerate's most profitable units and its divestiture represented one of the more interesting exceptions to the general rule that conglomerates keep their most profitable subsidiaries.

Virtually each step in the progress of this person and the corporation he heads can be explained by his quest for leadership. He has wanted, more than anything else in his business career, to be the head of an organization that would be recognized as the preeminent company in its field. He possesses considerable technical knowledge about the business he is working in. Nevertheless, many other people in the organization also have an excellent grasp of the technical aspects of the business, and technical skill is not the reason for his success.

The principal reason for his success, it appears to me, has been his desire to be responsible for people, not things. He has the ability to make people want to join him in working together, because the people who work for him believe, without question, that he will not do anything to hurt them personally or professionally. He has been able to lead people without their feeling that they were being exploited. That accomplishment is almost a paradox. Leadership always involves some type of exploitation of other persons, since anyone who is led gives up part of the self-direction of his or her talents.

I have watched him during negotiations. He sets a tone of light-hearted banter, which appears playful but also has serious, businesslike double meanings. As the negotiations proceed, he keeps summarizing his point of view and the point of view of the other party. As he does this, he positions himself as somebody who fully understands all of the points of view under discussion, and he appears as a person who does not have a narrow or a self-centered view.

Then, when the discussions reach an impasse, he turns to the person who holds a view that is most different from his, and he urges this person to see how his point of view will really be best. He never attempts to tell another person that he is wrong. He shows that another person's point of view needs to be changed because this person will gain more by doing so. There is an essential honesty that underlies the discussions. But most importantly, the emphasis is always personal and directed to the self-recognition of other people of what could be a greater personal benefit for them. I have never left bargaining discussions with this person without the feeling that I had observed the presence of a remarkable teacher who was really conducting a seminar in personal logic, in which business issues were almost incidental details.

A second person who has achieved a success in the maturity stage of the life cycle today owns a bicycle shop. The shop is, as bicycle shops go, very ordinary. It is relatively small in size and is terribly overcrowded. There are relatively few new bicycles for sale, and most new bicycles are in their shipping cartons to conserve space. Nearly one-half of the area of the shop is used for repairs, which is the mainstay of the business.

The business is always filled with people, and I always have to bide my time before I am waited on. Yet I never mind the delay, because I know that when I am served, no effort will be too much to help me. For example, if I need a matching nut to a bolt, someone will look through old tin cans to find what I need. This person turns away business regularly. He does not service makes of bicycles he does not sell, and if you have a make of bicycle that he does sell, but did not buy it from him, he will encourage you to take your repair business elsewhere. In short, he draws a very clear line between customers who qualify for his service and those who don't. But once you qualify, nothing is too good for you.

His success, I believe, lies in his ability to train a few repairmen how to make bicycle customers see that they and their bicycles really are one unit when the bicycle is in motion. He shows his repairmen how to repair and tune bicycles to their rider, and he makes sure that each bicycle receives the same care and attention it received when it was new. After a repair has been made, a repairman will often ride alongside a customer, to be sure that everything is right in operation, not simply in the shop.

The owner counsels his repairmen frequently, making detailed suggestions. The purpose of the suggestions is never to correct an error a repairman might be making, or to make a perfect repair or adjustment. Rather, the purpose is to help the repairman help the customer. The owner seldom speaks directly with customers, but works through his repairmen.

I have often seen signs saying that the customer is king or that customers are businesses' first concern, and I have sat through innumerable speeches that exhort people to serve customers better. But I have never seen customer service more effectively demonstrated. Nor have I seen a better example of personal leadership in working with an organization. The owner resembles a coach more than a doer, passing along his ideas to others who perform the tasks. He is, in simplest terms, an extraordinary teacher in one of the most mundane businesses on the street, bicycle repairing.

There is another example characteristic of the maturity stage of the life cycle, which is the other side of leadership. Persons in the maturity stage of the life cycle seldom seek to change the beliefs or institutions that inhabit the world. They have a respect for the established order. This is a time when religion becomes more important, because it represents an unchanging measure of humanity. During this period, an established neighborhood and long-standing friends provide a sense of continuity and stability. This is a conservative stage of the life cycle insofar as ideas and institutions are concerned.

.This stability of ideas and principles is essential to the success of the strong personal interest in other people. Persons in this period of their lives need the assurance that their beliefs are sound to give them the conviction that they need so that they might offer their help to others.

Thus the maturity stage of the life cycle passes on the torch in a broader sense. Persons in this period of their lives are the principal culture bearers of our society. They accept their culture. They also go a step beyond the acceptance of the adulthood stage. The maturity period vitalizes a culture, by rejuvenating the meaning of life. By caring for other people, people in the maturity stage find their culture to be a source of inspiration to themselves as well as to others. This is not a period when revolutionaries flourish. People in their maturity stage know too well that revolutions always end up requiring rigid principles that snuff out humanity. Without this humanity, there can be little caring for others or willingness to follow a personally liberating leadership.

Nevertheless, there is one aspect of the maturity stage of the life cycle that involves a severe attitude toward living. Most people in this stage of their lives force themselves to be highly selective in their use of time. This is a period for pruning the scope of activities. The days of exploring are behind. Now is the time for consolidating and evaluating.

One friend had undertaken a heavy schedule of local activities. This person had run successfully for city council and was active in a theatrical group. In addition, he had found time to watch a local soccer game which I was attending. I asked him how he managed to maintain all of his activities, as well as his insurance business, which I knew he had recently expanded. He said that he had become ruthless with his time and that he did only what really interested him.

He went on to say that he had trained a number of junior partners of his firm and now had time to work with the community.

I was struck by his use of the word ruthless in describing how he organized his time. He impressed me as being a considerate, almost a compassionate person. I wondered how he could be ruthless about anything, especially his time. He replied that he knew his strength had begun to ebb and that there wasn't enough time for anything except what was most important to him.

The need to be selective runs through this period of the life cycle as an underlying theme. There may be considerable generosity and affluence, but little of it is wasted unnecessarily. It is as if persons in this stage of their life cycle can see themselves as both an actor and a playwright and can blend the two roles together. Yet they also realize that their stage will be lit for only a limited period, and they do not have time to produce anything but the right performance for them. Anything more would be wasteful, and anything less would not pass along their torch.

Chapter 12

FINANCIAL STRATEGIES OF MATURITY: INVESTMENTS ARE YOUR STRENGTH

*T*HE period of maturity is a time of mastery. This is a time for sensing the right mode, the best circumstances where you can present yourself as you truly are, and do so in a confident manner. It is a time of doing less, but doing everything with efficiency and skill. Your physical strength is not as great as it was during earlier stages of your life cycle, but now you don't need to expend energy to be effective. You use skill more than force. In fact, the discovery that skill is superior to force might be regarded as one of the milestones of this period. That discovery has a profound effect. It renews hopes and serves as a source of renewed enthusiasm toward life.

There are five important financial strategies of maturity: (1) seek undervalued situations, (2) moderate leverage will help you, (3) become personally involved with tax issues, (4) keep hold of your savings rate, but be generous to yourself, (5) maintain one of the interests of the midlife stage.

The financial strategies of the maturity period are designed to enable you to make a major thrust toward expanding your financial base. These strategies are intended to conserve your energies and place a high premium on your being able to bring your experience into sharp focus, so whatever action you take is exactly as you intend it to be. They are also designed to minimize stress. Stress forces us into situations that bring forth extraordinary results, some good and some poor, but few predictable. By keeping stress low, you may perfect your financial skill in a controlled manner and anticipate your results with some accuracy.

This should be one of the tranquil periods of your life cycle in which to manage money. Your skill pays off, and if your skill is exceptional, your financial results are bound to be very good indeed. But even if they are not, you should find satisfaction from your money management.

KEY FINANCIAL GOALS OF MATURITY

You Should Seek Undervalued Situations

Your personal sense of well-being gives you new freedom to consider a wide range of investments. You have knowledge about business that is broader than ever before. Your judgment and skill are at a peak, and these talents give you the ability to look at unusual or speculative investments with a cool eye for the investment issues.

You now have the experience and judgment to penetrate confusing business matters and arrive at a clear conclusion. This attitude of mind gives you the ability to look beyond conventional investments and well-known companies. The financial markets are not perfect in their evaluation of securities and other assets. There are undervalued and overvalued investments. You are now in a better position to make these judgments than ever before. Moreover, the combination of illiquid, undervalued investments represent greatest risks and also the best investment opportunities. It requires a considerable amount of patience and steady effort to determine the opportunities from the risks, but patience and steady effort are traits that persons in their maturity stage of the life cycle understand.

These illiquid, undervalued investments include virtually all sound venture-capital situations, securities of companies that are down-graded for short-term reasons and companies that are about to go bankrupt. The ability to understand these business differences is a characteristic of many persons in this stage of the life cycle.

Moderate Leverage Will Help You

During the maturity stage of the life cycle leverage once again becomes important. High leverage was a characteristic of the adulthood stage, and in this stage you may have pushed leverage as far as your lenders would allow. Now, during your maturity stage, you will return to the use of leverage, but you will employ it more moderately.

Moderate leverage is important because you can now handle some risks of leverage, but you should not take extreme risks. Your interest in moderate leverage reflects a lessened opportunity to recover from possible losses. Before you make any investments, you should determine the line you draw between moderate or acceptable risks and what might be described as higher or unacceptable risks. Your ability to use leverage during your maturity stage of your life cycle reflects your regained stability and patience. Once again you are able to take a longer-term view toward investments, since your personal needs are not likely to suddenly change.

You have the perspective of a person who still has years of strength ahead. When you occasionally look at the years that you have accumulated, you may take a deep breath and wonder how many years you have left, and whether you should take any risks. But your sense of well-being quickly dispels those doubts. You have a solid insurance program. You aren't taking undue leverage risks, and you have a better capacity to judge investments than at any earlier period in your life cycle. You should step up to the mark, and swing your bat. You may not be able to hit as far, but you're a more consistent hitter than you have ever been. Those are important advantages that you should now utilize.

Become Personally Involved in Tax Planning

Tax planning at this stage of the life cycle becomes an issue of major importance. The effort to minimize taxes takes considerable time to explore. Taxes are not logical. They bear no relationship to any experience in business, science, the arts, or anything you have encountered. Taxes have been designed to take money from the successful, to help the less well off, and to provide incentives to participate in ways of life that the government thinks are good for you. They are like a powerful charity in which you must participate.

But you have considerable leeway in your mode of participation. To provide the right tax strategy, you should get involved in your taxes and develop a working knowledge of the tax codes. You need this knowledge to get a feel of the many tax issues that are important to you. There is no substitute for this hands-on knowledge. You should not leave the major tax issues to a tax professional, whether that person is a lawyer, an accountant, or a former IRS agent. You should make all tax decisions yourself, because they are basically personal decisions.

I have always believed each person in this stage of the life cycle should personally prepare his or her tax forms. Only in this manner are you sure to face tax issues squarely. You reach the basic issues of a tax decision when you write the figures in your own hand. You should consider professional tax specialists as your advisors. Let them make suggestions and ask them questions. But you are the person who should make the marks on the tax form.

Sometimes people will tell you that tax advisors can handle tax calculations more efficiently and accurately than you and that the IRS will be less likely to audit you if you use a CPA who is highly regarded by the tax authorities. These suggestions miss the point of your tax strategy in this stage, which is that you need first-hand experience to give you the background to make the right tax decisions.

Moreover, as soon as the tax advisor moves beyond the role of tax advising to the role of tax preparing, there is a conflict of interest. The IRS has virtually deputized the tax-preparing business by auditing returns of clients of tax preparers whom they believe are not acting in accordance with IRS preferences. Thus when a tax advisor prepares your return, you are, in effect, paying for a quasi-government official to do your work. It is difficult to obtain an independent advisory role from a tax expert in this arrangement.

Keep Hold of Your Savings Rate

This is a time to indulge yourself a bit. This does not mean that you should develop extravagant tastes, although some persons in this stage of the life cycle do this. Sometimes a woman will spend hundreds of dollars on a facial in an expensive salon in this period, when just a few years earlier, during her midlife stage, she clipped penny-saving coupons from local newspapers. Some men will do the same when they trade their Chevy Nova for a sports convertible.

Your tendency now is to be less frugal about how you appear. Your willingness to upgrade your appearance is a reflection of your rediscovered sense of well-being. You feel better during this stage of the life cycle, so you want to look better. You want to travel in better surroundings, and you want your image to be brighter.

In this stage you splurge from time to time. These splurges won't severely damage your budget or balance sheet if they are not too frequent and don't carry long-term commitments. The limit to your spending for consumption is your savings rate. As long as you keep savings at the level you believe is appropriate on long-term basis, you will be just fine. Earlier it was suggested that this level should be approximately 20 percent of your total income, and that ratio of savings to income continues to be a benchmark for you to consider.

Maintain One of the Interests of Your Midlife Stage

When you were in the midlife stage of your life cycle you found a treasure house of ideas and interests. You were not able to develop all the opportunities that flowed during that period. Now, in the maturity stage, you have carried forward the best ideas you discovered. But many of these interests have been placed on the sidelines, no longer as vital as they once were.

Look over these interests again. At least one of them deserves further exploration. In your maturity stage you can survey these remaining interests from a balanced perspective and evaluate them more concretely. These interests will again become important to you in the next stage of your life cycle. This is the time to maintain the interest, so that you season it with the insights of two periods of your life. That perspective will enhance the value of the interest in your next stage.

KEY INCOME AND EXPENSES CATEGORIES

Savings

You are likely to accommodate the increased tendency to splurge without hurting your savings rate, because your income will likely have risen from the preceding period. The relationship between consumption and savings will not involve the difficulties that occurred during your midlife stage of the life cycle. There is a fundamental reason you are able to handle consumption and savings as two compatible partners. You approach your consumption with more candor and objectivity than at any other period. You know what you are doing, and what you are doing is organized and controlled.

Some persons have started their own businesses or become head of the companies that employed them during the late midlife stage or early maturity stage of their life cycle. These persons will have opportunities to shift a portion of their increased consumption spending to pre-tax company expenses. In doing so, they may increase their consumption spending but find that consumption expenditures decline on an after-tax basis. That shift would make savings targets more manageable.

With consumption at a comfortable level, or at least at an acceptable level, you may find your attention directed toward the savings portion of your income statement. During this stage of your life cycle you have a powerful incentive to save. You are now in the afternoon of your life. You need to consider whether you will have the means to take care of yourself and your loved ones when your strength has left you. In the maturity stage of your life cycle you accept this prospect without being upset. You give attention to savings and make sure that there is a major place in your budget for this financial protection against future uncertainties.

Taxes

With a relatively high income, the maturity stage of the life cycle brings tax issues to the forefront of your financial situation. You will want to pay as few taxes as possible. This concern may lead you into financial directions that may be more complicated than you have ever faced. Few areas of your finances can get you into trouble quicker than improper tax-avoidance programs. The market for these programs has grown enormously in recent years, and many people have turned to the first program offered them as a solution to their tax problems. Some of these programs involve high and unrecognized risks, as well as long-term commitments that may not be in the best interests of the buyer.

In considering any tax avoidance program it is important to be sure that it does not go against IRS rulings or preferences. There are many gray areas in the field of tax deductions, and in many cases the IRS may frown on practices without actually disallowing the practice. For example, for many years some tax experts recommended that you should set up a small business and deduct the cost of one room of your house as a business expense in running the business. The IRS does not disallow deductions for the business use of a room in your house, but you need to have records that show not only that you derived income from the room, but that you set aside the room and used it only for business purposes. Moreover, according to informed opinion, if you use this tax deduction, your chances of an audit are greatly increased.

There are more fundamental issues in tax avoidance where you should use care. These issues involve long-term commitments of assets, and their problems may not emerge until years after the commitment is made. An example of this type of tax-avoidance program is tax shelters that defer taxes to a future date. A look at this type of tax shelter raises a number of problems that may not be completely reviewed at the time that the tax shelter is presented to you. The leveraged lease tax shelter defers taxes on the income from the lease until the term of the lease is completed. One advantage of this arrangement is that it permits an investor to deduct borrowing expenses to fund the lease from current income, while taxes on the income are postponed until the lease expires. There is a symmetry to this tax arrangement, since the tax effect of a deduction and earnings are balanced, only the time periods differ. The advantage of having immediate tax benefits and postponing tax payments appears appealing, particularly to persons who may have a large current tax liability and relatively little cash for payment.

But the piper must eventually be paid, and you do not know the financial condition you will be in when your tax liability comes due. If you have chosen a tax shelter because you are not able to reserve for current taxes or are reluctant or unable to borrow to cover that current liability, you may also be in a similar situation when your deferred tax liability comes due in the future. Then you would face not only the tax liability of that future year, but also the deferred tax liability. The result could be a considerable tax bill. One likely result of this situation would be for you to sign up for a new tax-deferred leveraged lease at a future time for the amount of that future tax liability. You would appear to solve your tax problem by keeping it postponed. On paper, your financial condition would look good, but you could not use an important part of your money.

In this process of trying to reduce your tax expense on your income statement, you also weakened your balance sheet. The borrowing you made to finance the lease used up part of your capacity to carry debt. There is no direct cost associated with using up your debt capacity, other than the interest payments. But there is an indirect cost, because you then would have reduced the options for other borrowing uses that you might wish to consider. Nobody knows what his or her future borrowing requirements will be. Perhaps you will use only a fraction of your borrowing capacity during the maturity stage of your life cycle. Yet unused borrowing capacity represents a valuable part of your financial situation and should be guarded carefully.

Leveraged lease tax shelters may become a pyramid of deferred taxes. The deferred tax liability would increase as each lease comes due, if you step up to progressively larger leases to avoid paying current taxes. This program is usually supported by the belief that a pyramid of tax shelters represents a good way of sheltering you from high tax rates during high-income years, enabling you to pay your taxes after you retire and your marginal tax rate declines.

The difficulties with this point of view are seldom discussed by salespeople and proponents of tax shelters. We have been living with a rising trend of inflation, which has steadily pushed up effective tax rates. This means that money buys less, but tax rates rise. For example, I would gladly take my current income, adjusted lower for price levels of 15 years ago, if prices were those of 15 years ago. I would then get the benefits of my current income with a lower real tax payment. The percentage of my gross income that would go to the government would be about one-quarter less.

Inflation has been accelerating, and the upward creep in real tax rates has been rising. If this accelerated trend should continue 15 years into the future, virtually everybody's retirement tax rate would be above, not below, the current tax rate. In arriving at that conclusion, assume that your retirement income would be half that of the final year of work, and the accelerated upward slope of the rate of inflation of the past 15 years, which rose from 3 percent to 12 percent, is extended for another 15 years, and Congress makes three 10 percent reductions in tax rates during the priod. The conclusion of this calculation is that deferred tax liabilities could cost you more by waiting. You may pay more tax by sheltering it.

Deferred tax shelters and pyramiding have a place in some people's financial portfolio, if they meet certain tests. First, the investment that the shelter is built around must be a sound investment. It must be able to earn income without involving significant risk. If the investment on which the tax shelter is based should falter, you would find yourself involved with more legal and accounting problems than you could imagine at the time you bought the shelter. I don't know of anybody who needs these kinds of problems.

Second, the person who undertakes a deferred tax shelter should build a reserve from after-tax income to offset the future tax liability. It is not enough to believe that the future tax liability would be paid from the earnings of the increase in the assets of the shelter. You simply don't know what the value of these future assets will be, but you do know that there will be a tax liability. The buildup of this reserve should not be regarded as an overly conservative financial position. Rather, it should be regarded as being realistic and doing what you would want to have done if you invested in a well-run corporation.

There are, of course, tax shelters that do not involve the issues of pyramiding. For example, if you are independently employed or are the principal stockholder in a private corporation, you will be able to set aside a significant part of your income in a pension trust fund, either IRA or Keogh. Contributions to this fund are tax deductible, and you may invest the funds in whatever assets you and your trustee believe are safe and likely to grow in value. You will pay taxes on income or principal as you receive it during your retirement. The matter should be kept simple, so you don't face any hidden future problem.

Beyond the simple tax shelters and retirement trust fund, such as a Keogh, IRA, or qualified pension plan, you are usually better off paying taxes in the year that they come due and keeping the after-tax surplus as part of your savings pool which is available for investment. The dollar totals on paper would be smaller than the totals you would see with tax-deferred programs, but the smaller totals would be all yours. You would be able to do virtually anything you wanted with those funds, and that flexibility could be a major advantage to you in the future.

Income From Your Work

Most persons who have worked throughout their adult lives are relatively content with the position that they hold and the income that they earn at this stage of their life cycle. These persons are mostly men, although an important number of women are in this category. Some persons have started their own businesses which have thrived, and others have continued working for or returned to a company as employees. Other persons have moved into positions as a senior specialist, a leading craftsman in a trade, or a position of respect as a worker. There is a feeling of well-being about work and income, and in most cases these people feel little incentive to go beyond the boundaries that circumscribe them. They are mainly interested in passing the torch of experience and helping others who are learning the skills that they perform proficiently.

At this stage the feeling of accomplishment you enjoy is rightfully yours. But there may be ways of making relatively small changes in the way that you do things that would increase the value of your work. You may wish to acquire a new skill that would reposition your experience in a useful way. That would represent adaptations to your work, not basic changes in your work. If you were to make such a change in the right way, you would likely find your value greatly enhanced and your income rise.

One friend was a salesperson for a pipe-fitting manufacturer. He had developed customers who relied on him for many years. He had given an excellent performance to the company, and he was regarded as being one of the stalwarts of the organization. He was an engineer by training, but he had not pursued education since his youth. He encouraged his son to enter engineering, and through his son's college course became interested in computers. He started to put his sales information into a small computer that he bought for his son's college work, and within a few months he mastered the skill of writing simple software programs. He asked the sales manager of the company if he could put other sales data into his home computer, in an effort to develop marketing information that might be useful to the firm. Within a year, he developed a system for quickly identifying changes in sales trends. This information was useful in product planning, production, and inventory control of the company. As the scope of work expanded, he trained one of the company's secretaries to post the sales data into the computer.

The sales manager left the company for another position, and this friend was promoted to become the new sales manager. His work with the computer gave him the winning edge for the promotion. Beginning as a hobby, this effort had become a major contribution to the company's development. He continued to serve his customers well, and he continued to be the same steady, reliable person he had always been. But his computer contribution, which was simple and basic, transformed his image from that of an excellent salesperson to an executive who thought like a marketing specialist. His income almost doubled, and he was much more valuable to his company.

This period of your life cycle fits perfectly with ways of upgrading your established skills. Any new skills that can be grafted to your core competence should enhance your value immensely. You would then combine a teacher's approach toward training other persons, a reliable and competent performer, and a mind that welcomed new ideas. This combination is unbeatable in business.

Your inclination will not be to embark on new directions, but if you should feel tempted to carry your efforts for newness to the point that they might interfere with your established work, you should proceed with caution. This is not the time to undertake a new career, no matter how tempting it might appear. You would not have the drive to carry you through all of the work you would need to complete.

Some people are given offers to join different companies during this period. These offers may be tempting, but they should be considered carefully. The change from one company to another would affect you more emotionally than at any earlier stage of your life cycle. During your maturity stage you need close personal relationships, and you need to help others in order for you to perform your best. If you lack these types of relationships, you will lose a certain charm and the illusive presence of a leader. You should protect this ambience that gives you value to an organization.

A change in companies would put you under a strain that you might not expect and dampen your performance. You might encounter less interest among persons in the new company to learn from your experience that you had expected or had been accustomed in your former company. The satisfaction you receive from your work might diminish appreciably. This satisfaction is important to you during your maturity phase of the life cycle. It is as valuable to you as money, perhaps more so, because you cannot perform at your peak without it. You should think twice, or even three times, about job offers from different companies, even when a considerable amount of money is involved.

Housing

In most instances housing expense declines in relative importance to other expenditures during this period. The typical person in the maturity stage of the life cycle bought a home or a condominium a number of years previously. Monthly mortagage payments would have remained steady, except for insurance and taxes, and income increased. The exceptions would be those persons who paid off their mortgage and found the elimination of mortgage payments to be a major windfall to their budget. Others rent or lease.

Each of these situations involves a different direction for the budget, but you should avoid any major increases in housing expense during the maturity stage of the life cycle. This is not the time to expand the size of your home, because children will be leaving, if they have not already left. This is also not the time to move to a more elegant home simply because you could now afford to make such a move.

You are likely to be established in your neighborhood and probably feel comfortable with nearby friends. Of course, there are exceptions, such as neighborhoods where property values are changing more rapidly than the average, or areas where safety has become a major issue. But for the most part, the stability that you have found in other areas of this stage of your life extends to your home. Unless your company transfers you, you are likely to remain where you presently live.

If you have paid off your mortgage, you may shift the funds that had gone to housing expenses to savings or to other investments such as securities. You may also use these funds for participation in a venture company. You may also consider buying a second home. In this case your monthly housing expenditures would not likely change very much, but the second home would become the focus of your principal housing expenditures. Second homes are usually bought for one of three reasons. They may be considered to be a future retirement home, a hedge against possible escalation of lawlessness in cities, or a tax shelter investment which earns rental income. You should review these reasons carefully before you purchase a second home.

The reasons for buying a second home that reflect future retirement aims or future fears about lawlessness involve a greater degree of risk than those that concern the earning power of the house as an investment. Many people anticipate their retirement needs in ways that turn out to be unrealistic. When these people actually retire they often find that a vacation home takes them away from their friends and activities which they wish to pursue. The fear that cities will disintegrate into jungle war may prove to be true, but events could also move in the other direction, and cities could become more civilized.

The maturity stage of the life cycle is a period when risk-taking of this type is not likely to fit well into your longer perspective. You may find that the fears that motivated you to make the decision to buy a second home may lose force over time. Unless the second home has value as an investment or has strong personal appeal, you may lose interest in it.

If you rent and should now wish to buy a home, choose a home that is inexpensive, well located to your work, with low upkeep. Most often, persons in the maturity stage who purchase their first home buy a condominium. Most people who have not owned a home and buy a home at this stage of their life cycle find that the expense of owning a home has a major impact on their budget. Because home buying represents asset building, the shift from rental payments to mortgage payments has the effect of increasing their contribution to their savings.

The maturity stage of your life cycle is a good time to buy a home if you do not already own one. Your budget can better accommodate higher costs of shelter, and you can better take on the responsibilities of increased leverage than during your previous stage of the life cycle. I have known a number of persons who bought their first homes during their maturity stage, and it was almost like seeing the enthusiasm of persons who bought their first home in the adulthood stage. The same pride and enjoyment appeared in the faces of these latter-day homeowners.

Earnings of Working Wives

This is the time for husbands to support their spouses in seeking a job if they have never worked. Until recently the majority of women in this stage of the life cycle have either not worked or have had limited work experience when they were much younger. It is important to give wives or women who are suddenly widowed or divorced the opportunity to develop the skills that the commercial world rewards, because the manner in which each of us relates to the commercial world provides an important part of our social and personal identity. Many women in this stage now find that their children have left home, and volunteer work doesn't test them to their fullest capabilities. They seek an opportunity to learn how they might fit into the commercial world.

There are practical as well as personal reasons to encourage this interest. The practical reasons include added income and are not the important reasons, except where financial survival is important. Working wives can incur added costs of clothes, transportation, and increased costs of food away from home, and these costs need to be subtracted from the added income. Perhaps the most important added cost is a higher incremental rate of your combined income taxes.

The personal reasons are the important ones for most women. Working is a way of self-fulfillment in our culture, once basic necessities have been provided. It is the means by which we develop and measure some of our best skills. To be shunted from this experience gives many women the feeling that they have not participated in the full range of their expression that may be available to them.

If you have not worked, or if you worked many years earlier, you need support from your family and friends. The door into the commercial world seems ordinary and commonplace to those who walk through that door daily, but to those who don't the step is really quite frightening. If you are not supported by your family, you may find the task of finding a job and working to be overwhelming. So it is important to get the support of your loved ones.

The first step is to find work that you would like to do. Perhaps you already have skills, and you can send out your resume and talk with prospective employers without delay. However, most women who plan to enter the job market lack current skills. A few courses at a local community college or a private trade school are quick ways of brushing up your old skills or learning new ones. Most private trade schools have an important advantage over community colleges, in that they usually have more effective placement services. Those schools are in business to get jobs for their graduates.

Your work should be an enriching experience. If you are not the principal source of income, you should seek work that does not involve unusual pressures, resolving conflicts between contentious people, or unusual hours. Your first job may not likely be your final job, but unless you have a favorable experience, you may be discouraged to look further.

An important characteristic of success among working wives as well as anybody who seeks employment, is finding the right boss. You will know quickly, probably during the first two minutes of your first interview, whether you like this person. If you have any doubts, keep looking elsewhere. You will learn more from your boss than anybody else on the job, and you need to find exactly the right person for you.

KEY ASSETS AND LIABILITIES

Securities

During your maturity stage, you will be better equipped to evaluate securities than at any previous period in your life cycle, and they are now an important vehicle for your savings. Your experience in the business world has spanned more than two decades. You have lived trough three or more business cycles. You have experienced major changes in the rate of inflation, pressures of business groups, union groups, minority groups, and several major wars. As you have lived through these developments, your background knowledge concerning financial markets grew deeper. You have learned to recognize that financial markets are a sensitive reflection of these economic and political developments.

You are able to evaluate securities during this stage of your life cycle with a candor that successful investing requires. The stability of the maturity stage of the life cycle provides for this objectivity. You are less swayed by surges of emotions or beliefs, and you have a sense of balance. Your sense of judgment, which you now trust more than ever before, is your best companion in investing.

The two broad areas of securities are stocks and bonds. Most people invest in stocks, because they usually can be purchased in smaller-sized units, usually from $5 to $50, and have traditionally been highly volatile. Thus stocks have provided an investor with greater opportunity for profit or loss. Bonds are usually much more expensive per unit than stocks and until recently have not fluctuated widely. Nevertheless, in recent years, the fluctuations of prices in bond markets have been larger than those of stock markets and have provided greater opportunities for gains or losses than stocks.

There are many guides for securities purchases and many methods of making selections. Nevertheless, I have found that there are five basic principles which have stood the test of time in all kinds of markets. People who have understood these principles and applied them have usually been successful in securities markets. These principles are particularly well suited to the experience and balanced temperament of persons in their maturity period of the life cycle.

First, interest rates provide the best, single indication of the financial effects of government financial policy. When you read in the newspaper that government programs are under way to increase government debt, increase inflation, and depress rewards for putting money in banks and other savings accounts, expect interest rates to rise and look for bond prices to decline. Conversely, programs that work to reduce inflation and encourage people to improve the productivity of the way they work will tend to lower inflation, and bond prices will tend to rise. All the information you need to know about these developments is on the front page of newspapers and is available to everybody.

Second, when you consider stocks you should look to the effect of future changes in real earnings on overall stock prices. Future real earnings include three factors, the future rate of reported earnings, the future rate of inflation, and the future corporate and personal tax rates. Stock prices are driven by earnings, and those three factors have proven to be keys to the future course of stock prices.

Reported earnings are the base on which investors assess the value of a stock. Stocks of companies that show prospects of providing a rapid future earnings expansion, particularly an unexpected spurt in earnings, are likely to show a better performance than other stock prices. The future rate of inflation is important in determining how valuable reported earnings will be. Higher rates of inflation reduce the future buying power of reported earnings and tend to depress stock prices. Tax rates affect the amount of earnings that a corporation can provide for itself and shareholders, as well as affect the amount of dividends that shareholders can keep for their own use. Changes in tax rates will change the value of earnings and dividends, and thus affect the value of stocks to shareholders.

You need to prepare your forecast of those three factors to look at the general level of stock prices. A combination of future higher reported earnings, lower inflation and lower tax rates will buoy stock prices. The converse would depress stock prices. You may think that you are at a disadvantage at making a valuation of these determinants of stock prices because you do not have a computer, and your only information is what you read in the newspaper. Don't worry, you are not at a disadvantage. It is your judgment of future trends, not mathematical computer programs, that is most essential, and you are at no disadvantage to computers.

Some investors in stocks follow fads in industries and regularly bid prices of stocks in industries up or down according to these beliefs. The fads are somewhat based on facts, but they are usually an exaggeration of facts and usually carry the future implications of facts way beyond a reasoned and critical understanding of what these facts imply. Thus investors often talk of growth industries or declining industries, as if the selection of the right type of industry will assure success in stock determination. When certain industries are in favor, stock prices of companies in these industries rise rapidly. But once an industry passes from favor, stock prices of companies in the industry turn weak. Sometimes, growth industries pass from favor quite quickly. I believe that more money has been lost in growth industries than in any other group of stocks.

Third, you should select individual stocks by using a number of simple but important indicators. These indicators would point with favor to stocks that showed a low price-earnings multiple, a five-year expansion in earnings which appeared to be accelerating and already exceeded the rate of inflation, better than average dividend, a return on equity that is in the upper quartile of stocks, and a relatively high ratio of current assets to current liabilities. This screen usually selects conservatively financed, basically profitable and often undervalued stocks. I have observed that over the past two decades that this approach has shown a good record.

Fourth, using whatever measure that you choose to select stocks, you should place buy and sell orders through a discount broker who executes its orders through an established major brokerage house. If you select stocks by yourself, there is no advantage to paying full-service brokerage fees. Over a period of years, these fees can represent a significant cost.

Fifth, bonds have recently become interesting to investors because of their recent sharp fluctuations in price. In screening bonds, plan to use Standard & Poor's and Moody's ratings as a guide for high-quality issues which have AAA, AA or A designations. You should not move below the single A rating, because lower ratings involve some speculative risk. Even with A and higher-rated securities, there may be uncertainties, because the rating services have sometimes not always been prompt in changing their quality designations. For example, these services did not blow the whistle prior to the bankruptcy of Penn Central, and some observers believe that these services continue to show reluctance to lower their quality designations as quickly as information becomes available which would indicate that they should do so. Other observers believe that rating services are caught in a conflict of interest and that they can never be completely responsive to downward changes in quality. These services are paid by securities underwriters and companies whose securities they rate.

Some investors have turned to bond mutual funds in hopes of finding professional managers who would work exclusively for the investor. If you invest in a bond fund, which pools a large number of bonds, you should check the ratings of the fund's portfolio. If you have any doubts about even one of the issues in the portfolio, avoid the fund completely. You don't want the double risk of a questionable issue and also a troubled financial intermediary between you and your money.

Metals and Minerals

Prices of most metals and minerals have risen sharply during the past decade. These include gold, silver, platinum, diamonds, and other less-well-recognized metals and minerals. Some observers believe that the past rapid rates of increase in these items will continue for the decade ahead, and these investments represent the key to future profits.

Inflation is the most important factor accounting for the sharp gains in prices of these metals and minerals. The underlying rate of inflation in the United States was virtually flat in 1960, rose to approximately 4 percent in 1970, and 12 percent in 1980. The acceleration in the rate of inflation over the past 20 years has worried many people more than the rate of inflation itself, and one response to this fear has been the purchase of easy-to-own precious commodities that retain or increase their buying power. The sharp, overall rise in prices of these commodities has further reinforced the belief in their value. The combination of fear of inflation and major gains in precious commodities has acted as a self-fulfilling prophecy of even more fear and gains.

A second reason for the sharp gains in prices of precious metals and minerals has been the instability of governments in many areas of the world. More than half a dozen countries have fallen into the Communist group in the decade of the 1970s. Revolutions in Central America and the Middle East have destroyed the work of millions of people. These developments have provided a strong incentive for large numbers of people to convert their wealth into coins and gems. This form of wealth can be easily concealed from tax agents of many newly formed governments. It is also a way of buying freedom to cross borders to escape political turmoil. These people have added to the demand for precious metals and minerals.

It would require the talents of a wizard to know for sure whether inflation and political turmoil will continue to grow in the years ahead. Investments in precious metals and minerals are really a speculative hedge against these uncertainties. If the world continues to move in the direction of the past two decades, the prices of gold, silver, platinum, diamonds, and many other precious commodities will likely rise even more rapidly than they have in the past. That world would be a very difficult world in which to live, but world disorder has been painfully frequent during the past millennium. In fact, periods of peace and steady prices have been the relatively rare periods.

It is, of course, possible that world problems will settle in the coming decade and governments will control budgets, taxes, and the supply of money in a way that will bring the rate of inflation down. That view may appear difficult to believe, in the light of past trends, but if it should occur, prices of precious commodities would show considerable declines.

Antique Investments

Antique investment is a hobby that has grown into the status of investment. Years ago, hobbies that involved collecting old objects were confined mainly to those persons who derived intrinsic value from their collection. The upward sweep of inflation has changed that. The fear that paper money will soon be worth much less has spilled over the market for precious commodities and has engulfed a wide range of tangible property that used to be considered almost worthless. It is as if the fear of inflation waved a wand over anything old and transformed that product into an object of scarcity and value. The recent flood of currency has been compensated by the recent shortage of antique investments.

Antiques have always existed among the rich. These people customarily enjoy their investments by sitting on 200-year-old dining room chairs, using 100-year-old sterling, and gazing upon 300-year-old oil paintings. Now, the middle class has sought a wide variety of objects to collect, including ash trays, porcelain dolls, American quilts, textiles, flower pots, and baseball cards. A recent auction of toy soldiers in London brought $60,000 for what was previously attic junk.

One friend collected model electric trains as a hobby, and over the years filled half of his basement with discarded trains. He carefully restored the trains whenever he could find parts. His hobby has now become one of his major assets, worth tens of thousands of dollars. One of his prize antique trains is a huge double-O gauge train that is almost large enough for a child to ride on. It is an interesting curiosity as it clicks and sputters around its track. Yet this collection of old metal and wire is almost worth its weight in gold.

Perhaps the most interesting development in collectibles has been the unusually rapid rise in the price of stamps. In fact, during the 1970s, the price increase of collector stamps has been almost identical to that of gold. Moreover, in an important aspect, stamps have been an even better type of collectible investment than gold, because prices of stamps have shown relatively little monthly fluctuation. The stability of stamp prices reflects their wide and diversified market and the large number of persons who hold stamps mainly for investment purposes.

I was made aware of the scope of the market for stamps when I traveled to the U.S.S.R. The border customs officer asked me to declare three specific items: books, gold, and stamps. I could understand why the Soviets wanted to censure books of incoming visitors, and I gathered that there would be a black market for gold. But I was puzzled about stamps. I was told, after I left the country, that gold is the ordinary man's international currency in the U.S.S.R., but stamps are the rich man's international currency. Unobtrusive, extremely portable, and in denominations and value that are not restricted by weight, stamps have become an important way money moves in and out of this and other countries that have rigid exchange controls.

Collectibles, gold, and other precious minerals share another common feature. They represent investments in markets in which transactions are largely unreported to government officials. In contrast, transactions in real estate and most securities are recorded, and any gain you may make from the sale of the investment is information that is automatically reported to state and federal tax authorities.

Investments in precious commodities and collectibles are seldom reported to government officials. If a transaction shows a capital gain, tax reporting is voluntary. The diversified and large number of buyers and sellers of these assets makes the establishment of government controls on these transactions unlikely in the future. Thus these assets have become the haven of many investors who, on political grounds, choose to avoid any involvement with government.

Insurance and Trusts

An important part of the fulfillment of the maturity stage is to pass on the torch and to provide the basis for continuity of your work through the development of other people. Your working relationships with other persons, particularly those who are embarking on their careers, is a major part of the personal rewards of this stage of the life cycle.

The financial side of this fulfillment involves insurance and estate planning. It is through these financial instruments that you can be sure that your personal wishes will be carried out if you should die. You are now in a period when your life expectancy is much shorter than it was in your previous stages. Thus these financial instruments need to be carefully considered during this stage of your life cycle.

Insurance is not new to you. You probably already have various types of insurance from your own purchases and your company's coverage. You also probably have a will from your adulthood or midlife period. Moreover, you are likely to have familiarity with the role that these financial instruments serve.

In previous periods, insurance or trusts may have played a major role to back you up. They were designed to stand in your place if you died. Their mission was primarily financial. If you died and didn't have enough money to leave your family, they might face a serious deterioration in their ability to accomplish the steps you hoped they would make. Insurance in particular was a financial supplement to the goals you felt were important for them.

During your maturity stage the role of insurance and trusts becomes less important as a financial substitute and becomes a vehicle of the way your hopes and wishes could be carried on if you become unable to carry them forward. Insurance and trusts now represent a continuation of your philosophy as much as a sum of money. That represents a major change in emphasis.

Your needs for life insurance will diminish during your maturity stage. If you are a person with a family, you no longer need life insurance to provide housing for your family and an education for your children in the event of your death. If you are a person without family requirements, your need for life insurance for personal purposes would continue to be minimal.

You may continue to need some life insurance, even if you perceive no immediate personal requirements. You may need insurance to pay estate taxes, or you may wish to leave money to persons who have helped you or to organizations that you believe could benefit from a contribution.

In the maturity stage term life insurance is usually afford-able, but if it is to be continued for many years, its premiums become quite high. A smaller amount of whole life insurance may be better, since you can lock in premium rates.

You should look carefully at your disability insurance coverage. In addition, if you have accumulated net assets of more than $100,000 or have an income of $25,000 or more, you should look at your liability insurance. These types of insurance are often overlooked during this period of the life cycle.

Disability insurance is coverage against the possibility that you will remain alive, but you could be unable to work, and possibly require some ongoing medical or other help. This help is almost always costly, and disabilities can some-times involve long periods. If you work for a large corporation, you are probably covered with some type of disability insurance, but you should review your coverage anyway. If you are self-employed or work for a small company which has few employee benefits, you should look at your disability insurance needs carefully.

Disability insurance is important during this stage of the life cycle, because health becomes a problem for many persons in this period. In fact, less than half of the persons which might be eligible to retire at age 65 ever do so because they have already left the work force. Some retire early, preferring to leave work with reduced benefits. Others retire early with cash incentives to do so. But a large number of persons leave the work force in the maturity stage because they can no longer work. Some receive no company retirement benefits, either because there are none, because they are not old enough to qualify, or because they have not worked long enough in a particular job to qualify.

A second area of insurance you should review is liability coverage. Persons in the maturity stage often have built up considerable assets, and inflation has increased the value of these assets to levels that are well above their purchase price. Moreover, in many cases the income of persons in this age group is relatively high. You have become a lawyer's dream, if you should be liable for damages. Automobile accidents are a common cause for being sued, but people still slip and fall on door steps. You should be sure that your total liability insurance is high enough to cover you against an almost unbelievable number of contingencies. You should not forget that the greater your assets, the more likely you would be sued, if something unfortunate happened.

You may wish to consider the use of trusts during your maturity stage. They can provide you with a way that your philosophy can be carried forward in your absence. They usually provide a human interpretation of your wishes, so that the words you might say are actually said. Somebody takes your place and serves as a representative of the way you look at matters. Money, of course, is the vehicle by which this is accomplished, but the principal issue, so far as your personal interests are concerned, is your personal philosophy.

Many financial issues are involved in trusts and estates. They are an effective form of tax shelter. But trusts and estates usually involve a loss of control over the assets that are covered by these legal instruments. Trusts and estates that provide for greater tax benefits also involve a surrender of control over the assets. The issue of control is important from a money-management point of view, because you may want to use these assets at a later period of your life cycle for purposes you can't now imagine, and these future needs may represent an important constraint to your use of trusts.

For these reasons, trusts are usually a difficult issue to resolve, even if you have built up considerable assets. You should take plenty of time if you consider them. They involve emotional issues, and your use of trusts and estates reflects your willingness to hand over the control of an important part of your assets to another person.

If you are interested in using these legal instruments, start with a small trust or estate. Observe how you feel about it over a fairly long period of time before you move further. You may wish to set a minimum of two years for this trial period. Some trusts last for a designated period, and you can get back control of your assets at that time. Consider how difficult or easy the trust is to live with, and note your feelings toward the trust or estate.

Finally, you should keep in mind that you have one more important stage in your life cycle, and this stage will probably add to any strain you may presently feel about a loss of control over your assets. Don't let impulse carry you too far. Keep a considerable amount of flexibility in the control of your assets, so that you will be able to fulfill the challenges of the next stage of your life cycle.

Chapter 13

AGE AND SIMPLICITY:
AGE 66 AND ONWARD

*T*HIS period is probably the most misunderstood stage of the life cycle. It is a period of tension, yet with that tension brings the possibility of personal development that far outdistances the development of earlier periods. The tension reflects the debilitating physical effects of age against an insurgent intuitive energy. From that tension comes simplicity and a new type of personal enrichment.

The usual impression of this stage of the life cycle is quite different. Age is widely regarded as being a period of calmness, withering strength, and a fading personality. It is the period when our culture puts people out to pasture. We no longer expect these people to produce anything. At best we try to treat them nicely, even indulge them a bit, like we might treat children. We have tended to overlook the special kind of insight that is provided by persons in this stage of the life cycle. The insight that these people show is very tough and durable. They winnow their effort and concentrate on only the most important issues. They learn how to withstand stress by simplifying their work.

It is no accident that Germany developed into a powerful anti-Communist nation under a man in the age and simplicity stage of his life cycle. Konrad Adenauer was 73 years of age when his party won the first Bundestag election in 1949, and he became chancellor. He supported a sharp change in the prevailing socialist thought of the time and provided an economic policy that supported free markets. He started the movement to reconcile Germany's differences with France, and he provided direction to the people of Germany that enabled them to see the benefits of remaining free, rather than compromising or turning to communism. This was an achievement for the times, since it involved the re-energizing of a weary, defeated, and demoralized people who had lost a war as well as half of a nation four years previously. A more youthful, more vigorous person probably couldn't have done the job, because the issue at stake was primarily philosophical and required the simplicity that a philosophical outlook was based on.

The case of Charles de Gaulle also illustrates this point. If this leader had died when he was 65 years of age, he would have been remembered as a minor commander of a minor army in a major war. However, when he was 68 years of age, he became premier of France during the most difficult period of that country's post-war period. France was deeply divided concerning its role in the Western alliance and its colony of Algeria. The latter issue had to come to a crisis point. I was visiting France during this period, and the passion that people felt at the time was little appreciated elsewhere. It was a parallel of the problem the British now face with Northern Ireland. In both instances, settlers had taken up homesteads, developed the country, and the mother country felt a patriotic duty to hold on to the colony.

De Gaulle separated Algeria from France and turned to the development of an independent military defense system outside the North Atlantic Treaty Alliance. The settling of the Algerian issue freed the French from a costly diversion of their money and manpower and allowed France to concentrate on the larger issue of building its economic strength.

The issue, when viewed in this light, was simple. The development of an independent and anti-Communist military force foreshadowed the need for all of the nations of the free world to begin the same task as this burden subsequently began to weigh heavily on the United States. It is easy to forget that these unusual and strenuous decisions were made by a man who, according to customary retirement policy, would have been relegated to a life of isolation from the working world. Yet in the light of two decades, the decisions were correct for France and prophetic of the political situation that the free world would be groping toward.

One of the nation's leading college football coaches provides another example of the unusual resources of this stage of the life cycle. After he passed 65 years of age, this person's ability to win football games was understood as reflecting more than luck, enthusiasm, and half-time exhortations. One of his recent defensive ends said that "there is never much rah rah talk, just plain common sense. In that respect, he's one of my best philosophers of life I've ever met." This is not simply the reaction of an impressionable youth. This person does not dominate meetings by power or force, but by something quite different. He senses what is important and engages his powers of intuition to reduce problems to simple and practical solutions. He rarely raises his voice and talks slowly. His power is something more than energy, logic, or any of the talents that characterize the previous stages of the life cycle.

I once worked with a similar type of person in the business world. This man was 65 years of age when I first met him, and he and I worked together over the following four years on a strategic planning project for a division of an international chemical company. He was one of the most skilled businessmen I have met. He managed a group of six small specialty refractory companies in an economically depressed area of southern Ohio, with customers in two declining businesses, the steel and pottery industries. His group of companies should have been bankrupt, given their business situation. Several competitors had closed their doors, and others were in financial difficulties.

When I first met this person, he was trying to accomplish two tasks. The first was easy for him, involving the organization of these recently acquired companies. The second was more difficult, involving ways of convincing the senior management of the central corporation not to retire him. For four years he succeeded in both objectives. As I reviewed his operations, he appeared to break every rule for profitability, except one. His equipment was obsolete, his work force was relatively low skilled, his buildings were made from wood and were at least 100 years old, and he had no research-and-development or quality control departments. However, he skillfully improved his products so that they were perceived as being superior by customers, and he priced them so that he and his customers shared in his improvements.

As I looked deeper into his operations, I was struck with the way he had challenged the abilities of an essentially unskilled work force. The productivity of his operations was more than double that of his competitors. Most importantly, nobody felt exploited or pushed. There were no answers to the question of why this occurred in the financial and production data that I looked at, so I asked plant managers if I could speak directly with workers on the line. I spoke with perhaps a dozen line workers and was impressed with the respect they all held for the head of the division. The workers felt that they could make suggestions to improve matters and that they would be remembered personally by him. Moreover, they felt that he would guide them so that they could keep their jobs, when their friends and neighbors were losing theirs.

This person had turned much of his operation into a development laboratory as well as maintained it as a production facility. He had done this by knowing the particular skills of workers and making them proud to be innovative. Their concern for workmanship was reflected in the high levels of productivity.

This stage of the life cycle enables you to put together the threads of lost hopes. You have had two earlier periods when this outlook has been before you. During your adolescent stage you learned about yourself emotionally. During your midlife stage you fathomed your thinking. In the age and simplicity stage you explore your intuition and use it as a capstone to bring all of these understandings together in a uniquely personal expression. Your intuition provides simplicity to your understanding of yourself.

The examples noted earlier show that simplicity in the way you view matters does not necessarily involve a passive attitude toward life. Each of the illustrations involved men who were very much the center of their stage. These persons showed that they used their mental powers more fully during this stage than in previous years. Each had been active in younger years, but they became more focused during the age and simplicity stage of their life cycle.

Not everybody needs to be active to be effective. Some personable and charming people are quiet, other persons are gifted in science or art and are difficult to approach. They all can be effective in communicating their purpose to others. What is special about this stage of the life cycle is the opportunity to focus your special talents, refine them, and simplify them. You can then use these talents more effectively than at any other period of your life cycle.

Simplicity has a special effect on people in other stages of their life cycle. It provides a way of focusing the energies of the adulthood stage, guiding the teaching skills of the maturity stage, and harmonizing the discoveries of the adolescent stage.

Yet our society is not organized to utilize the talents of the age and simplicity stage of the life cycle. We have built our work force around an age bracket that begins from 18 to 25 years of age and usually ends before 65 years of age. We push these people to the forefront of work, and through our Social Security and retirement programs, financially penalize anybody who chooses to work beyond that point. The persons who work into their age and simplicity period have included a number of remarkable individuals who have persisted against the tide of social and financial custom.

Health is often given as the reason a person takes early retirement or chooses to stop working. In many cases, there is a major deterioration in the health of persons in the age and simplicity age group. Yet a close look at many of the persons who have continued to work into this stage of the life cycle shows that their health has also deteriorated and that they, too, suffer from a weakened physical makeup. There are many debilitating diseases that have the effect of sapping the energy and the will to persevere.

Equally important, however, is the interest in continuing to persevere despite weakened health. Many people in this stage of the life cycle find that their physical weakness acts as an incentive to pull together their remaining powers of the mind, and they learn how to allocate their lessened resources more efficiently. Often, the sense of belonging to a group and a feeling of self-esteem from the group serves to reinforce the commitment and the strength of persons in this stage. These people are the most efficient users of their lives of any stage of the life cycle. The easy days of unlimited time of earlier stages of the life cycle are gone, and the limit of time and resources sharpens the focus of these people.

The focus does not have the power or drive behind it that occurred in the midlife stage. Now, the focus almost appears by itself. It is as if these people give a nudge to their lives, and the pieces fit together. The age and simplicity stage of the life cycle uses different means of achieving its end than the resolve that comes from willpower. It uses a sense of detachment and an intuitive recognition of what needs to be accomplished.

There is another approach toward health which many persons in the age and simplicity stage have pursued. These people have come to regard their health as a matter that is partially under their control. They recognize that there are limits to their health, and they stay on the protected side of those limits. They have learned how to pace their efforts, so that they may work in a smooth manner. They avoid upsets, and they know the wearing effect of stress. They have learned how to avoid situations that put them in a position in which they must act but cannot control the outcome.

Perhaps no issue is more important to this stage of the life cycle than the challenge of how to handle a weakening physical body. You must accept the fact that you have become physically weaker. At this stage you cannot master your health, but you can accommodate it. A person who is 65 years of age cannot work as hard as he or she could when he was 35. If you cannot gracefully reduce your workload, you will be required to drive yourself mercilessly to keep your workload as high as it was. If you do that, your health surely will break.

The deterioration of the physical body cannot be stopped. Sometimes a minimum rate of deterioration is a very slow pace, and other times it is not. The actual rate of deterioration is not as important as the way that change is perceived. If the decline is accepted, there is a growth of personal control that outpaces any display of strength that accompanied the earlier stages of the life cycle.

Perhaps the most difficult challenge of this stage is the one in which a person learns that the number of months or days of life are numbered. Most persons never spend much time thinking about how long they may live. I have looked at life expectancy tables hundreds of times over the past years, and I usually look to see how many years I have left. But I never consider the information seriously. I know that the issue is important, and for that reason, own life insurance. Yet, I—and most other people—do not dwell on the gravity of the situation.

All of this detachment disappears suddenly when there is a short-term number for the amount of time that may be left. The observers of many terminally ill persons have noted that the typical reaction to the news involves the five reactions of denial and isolation, anger, bargaining, depression, and finally acceptance. This progression represents a compressed journey of the reactions that each person comes to recognize more gradually as part of the process of aging. Most persons have the luxury of taking their time in working through their understanding of these issues, and even taking a detached view.

Facing the imminent prospect of leaving life brings the issue of simplicity abruptly to the fore. There can then be no denying of this inevitability. One of the common characteristics of those who have reached the acceptance state has been a closeness of people who cared, a putting in order of their most important wishes for remembrances, and a wish to surround themselves with their most familiar sights, such as their furniture, pictures, and a favorite view from a window. All of these represent the quintessence of simplicity. It is as if the person were asked what, above all, was most enjoyed and pleasurable. Out of this simplicity often comes a new feeling of lessened worry over one's death. In fact, among a few people, the worry over death becomes almost insignificant, and the concern for others becomes a major concern.

The worst mistake anyone can make during this stage of the life cycle is to stop working. Perhaps retirement may force you to stop your past work, but there are always other types of work that are available. Work can include the development of a hobby that you kept on the back burner during a previous stage of the life cycle. It can include volunteer work in a hospital or church work. But work is important, because it gives you the material you need to develop your skills of this period. Without work, you will feel a sense of incompleteness, a quest without a purpose. This sometimes leads to a deep frustration, which persons in this stage of the life cycle cannot handle well. Two stories will illustrate this.

A friend who had been very helpful to me in getting a college scholarship spent the ten years of his retirement in luxurious consumption. Before his retirement he had been a successful executive in a major corporation, and on his retirement, he was suddenly without a job. He tried to fill his time with various kinds of volunteer work, but whenever I visited him, he seemed a bit bored with this work. His wife died, and then quite unexpectedly, his only daughter became ill. I was concerned about him, and I called on him. He was deeply saddened. In his retirement, he had tried to keep up his way of life as a corporate executive, but this was now an empty dream. The loss of his two loved ones brought home to him the realization that his years had been misdirected.

A close friend of the family was a professional nanny to children. She also wrote poetry. The poetry was always about popular subjects. During World War II she wrote about patriotism. During subsequent years her poems were cleverly humorous, and in recent years, her poems, which we receive as Christmas cards, have been about loyalty and faith. She and her husband, who has died, were never able to afford more than the next month's rent and a good meal once in a while. Yet she kept ends together, and she tells me that she works diligently every day on her poetry. Her glasses are thick, so this work has to be limited. But that limitation has not hindered her, since she now develops her poetry in her mind more than she did when her vision was better.

She has risen above her physical impairments through her writing. She considers herself to be a working person, and she views her friends as poetry listeners who need to hear what her poems are discussing. She has given herself a marvelous job, and her life has become richer as she has simplified it.

Both of the persons in these two examples faced the same problems of growing old. Both lost loved ones. One pursued a way of spending and living that was more typical of an earlier stage of the life cycle, the other pursued the work of a lifetime. One had great amounts of money and used this money almost as a substitute for ebbing physical strength. The other had no money and faced the issues of advancing age.

This is not to suggest that money is not important in the age and simplicity stage of the life cycle. Poverty and old age are not a blessing, but they are not necessarily a curse. The sadness of old age may not be a lack of money as much as misuse of money to sustain a period of life that has passed.

In the previous stage of the life cycle, the maturity stage, there is often an impression of an easing in the energies of the mind, as weaknesses of the body become more apparent. In the age and simplicity stage of the life cycle the physical condition of the body continues to give way to time, but there appears to be an upwelling of intuition in ways that never appeared before. People have frequently described this development, often using different terms. Sometimes they speak of their increased interest in their spiritual life. Others talk about their being able to understand how matters fit together in ways that their intelligence or emotions had not shown them. Intuition, the ability to look behind our knowledge to see meanings that are not directly observable, is another term for these descriptions. It would be a mistake to neglect this outpouring of intuitive energy or to waste it on anything except what is most important to you. This energy is perhaps the most vital and personal energy you have ever experienced. This intuitive energy does not have the power of your emotional energy, or even of the intellectual energy of your earlier stages of the life cycle. It is more subtle and requires a simple life for its nature. This energy is like the water of an oasis in the desert. Whatever it touches turns to life and blooms, but there is not much of it.

The increased interest in the intuitive capacities is not always acknowledged. My friend who spent his final decade trying to live in a style of another period of his life appeared to be unmoved by his intuitive stirrings. His difficulty in meeting his deep personal crisis was no doubt made more difficult because he had not developed these new skills. The denial of these intuitive abilities often leads to frustration and sometimes a withdrawal from friends and family. This is a sadness that is perhaps greater than death, because it represents a potential for renewed life that instead is left to wither.

The development of intuitive abilities of this stage of the life cycle are important to the emphasis of simplicity in this period. Hard-pressed activities involving considerable stress crowd out intuition. Whenever we are under emotional or intellectual pressure, we put blinders on our imagination and tend to confine ourselves to the established ways of solving our problems. I have seen great accomplishments of people under stress, but not results that appeared to reflect intuition. The results showed the effects of only determination, skill, power, and knowledge.

Intuition needs a more passive environment to flourish, and this stage of the life cycle requires simplicity to allow your intuitive abilities to bloom. This is a period of your life when you need to have some time to relax, and time each day to let your mind select what it wants to consider. You would be astounded at the insights and discoveries that come to you.

There are two characteristics of the language of people who have understood the challenge of the age and simplicity stage of the life cycle. The first is that people in this period of their lives tend to be economical in their use of language. They choose their words more carefully than persons in other stages of the life cycle. They think of language as a barrier as well as a bridge to understanding. It is a barrier in the sense that while they are talking, they do not have an opportunity to reflect on the issues or conversation. Their economical use of words gives them a few extra moments in a discussion to reflect, to use their intuitive faculties to understand the meaning of the discussion.

I once interviewed a senior diplomat who was in his eighties. The interview was intended to be perfunctory, since this man's views are no longer important to the course of political events. Nevertheless, the organization that I worked for felt their proposal would be viewed with more favor if his name were associated with it. I had met this person 25 years earlier as a student when he was at the height of his political power.

My interview was a complete surprise. I had expected a somewhat rambling and disjointed review of commonly known facts and opinions, much as he had regularly expressed himself years earlier. Instead, he spoke slowly, with short sentences and carefully chosen words. Moreover, he always went right to the point and quickly said exactly what he wanted to say. He often paused and allowed frequent moments of silence. I was struck with the change that had occurred, and I wondered whether my memory had been faulty. I asked people who remembered this person from earlier years, and I am convinced that my memory is accurate on this point. There is no question that this person had undergone a remarkable development in his age and simplicity stage of the life cycle. I regret that he is not now at the height of his political power.

A second characteristic of the language of persons in this stage of their life cycle is that they frequently use old sayings to illustrate their points. These epigrams are seldom used as frequently in the earlier stages of the life cycle. During those earlier stages, the old sayings would make the user appear untechnical, simplistic, or unknowledgeable. However, persons in the age and simplicity stage do not wish to appear so highly structured or overbearing. They prefer the quickness, lightness, and simplicity of an adage to convey their thought.

The use of old sayings also conveys a sense of being a part of a long tradition, and this has a settling effect on the listener. This preference for old sayings is in the literature of many writers. A good example is Cervantes when he was in this stage of his life cycle. Some of his last writing consists of a series of old sayings, one right after the other. These represent one of the best collections of adages I have ever seen, but they are so skillfully used that they appear as ordinary conversation.

Some form of work is often useful to develop your intuition and style of simplicity. A key aspect of work involves your relationship with other persons, and you need these relationships. It is through people that you interpret your efforts. They provide observations and opinions, and these comments serve to keep your efforts useful.

There is sometimes a tendency for people in their age and simplicity stage to withdraw from life too much, to reflect too intensely. Those people may literally sink in their thoughts. Nevertheless, I have observed that people in this stage who have moderate work or have set themselves tasks are better able to keep a sense of balance to their lives than those who don't have some form of pursuit. During this period, a task that needs to be done has kept many people alive and well, in addition to having given them personal enrichment. It is a challenge to find the right tasks, but if they are found, the personal achievement of this stage of the life cycle can be the finest of all.

Chapter 14

FINANCIAL STRATEGIES OF AGE: A TIME FOR SIMPLICITY

*T*HE period of age requires a steady hand at the wheel, since you are again challenged in a fundamental way. In this stage of the life cycle, you balance two different financial directions. You need financial security, since you do not know how long you will live or whether you will face unusual expenses in future years. Yet this is also an exciting stage of your life cycle, and you may explore new areas of interest that you had never dreamed of considering.

There are five key financial strategies for this period: (1) income should be spent as it is received, (2) leverage should be reduced or eliminated, (3) your health insurance coverage should be comprehensive, (4) tax and estate planning should be kept current, and (5) your liquidity should enable you to meet an emergency.

During this period you will use these strategies to implement the broad issues of security and personal enrichment. Your skill in weaving these financial strategies into those two broad personal needs represents the challenge for this period of life. Your success in meeting that challenge will largely reflect the simplicity that you use in organizing your life and getting rid of all encumbrances that you no longer need.

KEY FINANCIAL GOALS OF AGE

I once asked a highly regarded economist at a major eastern university how much a retired person should spend of income and principal on a monthly basis. His answer was that the person should spend whatever would be necessary to bring assets to one dollar on the day of this person's death. Despite the apparent flippant tone, this answer implies the need for personal enrichment along with the need for security. The answer suggests that money you have not spent on yourself has been inefficiently used, so far as you are concerned. Once you have taken care of your obligations, your final years should be as full as possible. To the extent that money can enhance this enrichment, you should use it. Of course, the difficulty of the economist's answer is that nobody knows exactly how long he or she will live. Thus persons in this period need to keep a cushion between their spending and their assets.

Income Should Be Spent as It Is Received

This is the stage of your life cycle when you can "travel light." Traveling light means that you can look at expenses the same way you did when you were an adolescent. You don't need to stay at exclusive hotels when you travel, as you may have done during your maturity stage. Now, you can stay at inexpensive guest houses or with friends, as you might have done when you were in your teens. It means seeking out what is of particular interest to you and finding an inexpensive way of enjoying that interest.

One friend told me that she had always wanted to find out who her ancestors were, and when she retired, she traveled to Ireland to walk over the ground her family had walked centuries earlier. Although she had accumulated considerable wealth, she chose to travel inexpensively with a small suitcase she could carry herself. She remarked how she would have traveled 10 years earlier. Then she would have insisted on first-class accommodations. Now she felt her way of traveling light would be more fun and would be closer to the family people she was interested in meeting. In many ways, she resembled her teenage granddaughter more than her daughter.

Traveling light is also a state of mind which reflects the importance of simplicity in this stage of the life cycle. It means that you should get rid of whatever you no longer use or need. The ideas that identified your status or position in your maturity stage are no longer important, and you should free yourself from them. You should clean out your thinking as you clean out your wardrobe. And after you have done that, you should look toward your renewed personal development.

Leverage Should Be Reduced or Eliminated

Leverage involves risk, sometimes a long-term horizon for fulfillment. In this stage of your life cycle you should avoid high risks or long payout periods. Your personal needs are more immediate, and you need to be able to plan on your resources.

Leverage is not purely a financial matter. It can add to your worry over risk and divert attention from your personal interests. It affects how you look at yourself. Moreover, you probably have little need for leverage at this time. Whatever your financial situation, there is likely to be some way of life that can accommodate your level of income and enable you to pursue your personal interests.

You most likely should not renew leverage commitments when they are terminated. Some leverage arrangements involve heavy tax payments when they are completed. You will pay the taxes and walk away. It sometimes appears easier to further postpone tax liabilities than to pay the piper. If you take the easier route, you will not simplify your financial situation. Any program that does not simplify your income statement and balance sheet will eventually exact a steep price from you in the way that you think and reflect on your mode of living. It will take time and energy away from other interests that you have a major inclination in pursuing, and you should remember that you no longer have time to do anything except what is most important.

Insurance Coverage Should Be Comprehensive

Retirement often brings a major change in your insurance coverage. If you worked for a large company, your insurance coverage was probably fairly broad and included personal disability and health coverage. Many companies provide elective insurance coverage for retirement employees. These programs offer insurance at group rates, or at subsidized rates below the rates paid by persons buying insurance on an individual basis. Usually, these programs offer health and sometimes term life insurance. If these insurance programs are available, you should consider signing up for them.

Health insurance is your major concern. Your health coverage likely fits into one of three categories. First, you may have virtually no private coverage, and if you become ill, you would rely on county or public health programs. Second, you may have private coverage that covers some, but not all health contingencies. The exceptions would involve costly expenses that would have to be paid by you. Third, you may be completely covered, and whatever might happen to your health, your income and assets would not be affected. You should avoid the second situation. This position exposes your future income and assets literally to confiscation, if you are unfortunate to suffer a lingering and debilitating disease that requires expensive treatment.

The difficulty with buying sufficient additional health insurance is that many budgets would then be severely squeezed. Faced with this dilemma, some people have chosen to hide their assets so that they are not part of the public record such as gold, silver, diamonds, or funds held outside the country. As the squeeze of inflation has eroded the buying power of retirement income, the temptation to choose this route has become greater. Yet I would avoid it at all costs, because this response will make your life more complicated, not simpler. You should pay the health insurance costs. You then eliminate a financial worry that, if you should become ill for a prolonged period, could become a problem of enormous magnitude to you.

The other type of insurance that you should review is life insurance. Your need for life insurance at this stage of the life cycle is less than during earlier stages, when life insurance was a way of providing a cushion against loss to others. Now, the need for the cushion is much diminished, largely consisting of a way of providing for the surviving spouse, if a company pension were to stop with the death of the covered worker. Often, this contingency is covered by insurance that is already in force.

A second important reason for life insurance in this stage of the life cycle is estate taxes. In recent years, inflation has pushed the value of the estates of many persons into relatively high estate tax brackets. The problem has become particularly acute with farmers, although it would also include many independent business people. Life insurance may be important to pay the estate taxes, so that at the time of death, assets do not have to be sold for tax purposes.

Tax and Estate Planning Should Be Kept Current

You should have a professional tax specialist review your overall tax and perhaps your estate situation. This audit should not require prolonged services or an extensive fee. You might wish to ask more than one tax specialist for an estimate of the charge for review. I know one accountant who feels so confident that she can save money for people in this situation that she says that she will send no bill for her fees if she cannot find tax and estate solutions that would save her clients at least four times her hourly rate. This is an interesting marketing approach, and according to her, she has always presented her bill.

You should not expect that tax and estate matters will be simple in their procedures, but you should require the results of tax and estate matters to be simple. You should not permit these matters to become complex and difficult to live with. If you feel that matters are becoming complicated, find a tax advisor who can simplify them. If tax and estate planning becomes complicated, it can involve large fees, and you may find that you are more bothered than helped.

Liquidity Should Enable You To Meet an Emergency

The age and simplicity stage of the life cycle involves a greater possibility of sudden personal and financial emergencies than any other stage of the life cycle. Your health may be fine at the moment, but it is also more fragile than in any other period. Moreover, you may represent a major source of assistance to other members of your family who may have unexpected financial needs. Your son or daughter may be laid off work or want to start a new business. A grandchild may be unable to return to college without financial help. There are all kinds of unexpected needs, and often you will learn of them at the last moment.

Whenever emergencies arrive, there is usually little time to find buyers or lenders for illiquid assets. At these times you need to be able to give your time, advice or comfort. Thus some part of your assets should be available for use within a few hours. Two or three bank credit cards with high upper borrowing limits and a savings and checking account with automatic switchover of funds from the savings account can provide this liquidity. Some persons feel more comfortable with more liquidity. Liquidity usually involves a lost opportunity for interest, dividend, or other income. But it also adds to the simplicity of your life, and for this reason, it has value.

KEY INCOME AND EXPENSE CATEGORIES

Education

Once again, as in your adolescence and midlife stage, you should be prepared to spend to develop your talents through education in its broadest meaning. The education may be from books, lectures, courses, study groups, religious or educational institutions, as well as your own meditation. Some persons in this stage of their life cycle look upon travel and learning about a wide variety of different ways of living as their quest. Others consider writing songs or taking art or drawing lessons. Some persons return to a musical instrument they discontinued years earlier. Physical fitness attracts others, and I have met many people who have started tennis in their sixties or joined a swim club for regular exercise. The variety of interests is almost endless.

The costs involved with education in this stage of the life cycle should not be large and should not be a limiting factor to your participation. This is a period when education is stripped of its social and employment benefits. It is now concerned with the original meaning of the word, which is to lead someone to a better understanding of himself or herself.

You should find someone in your field of interest who can lead you and inspire you to move ahead in your learning. Your criteria for choosing this person will be different from what it was during your earlier years. In those earlier days you usually looked for someone who was recognized as an expert and had an enormous amount of information. Now you should look for someone who has sense of meaning toward work that is personal and intrinsic. You are now looking for a personal core in any technical skill that you acquire. You will want to find somebody who recognizes that developing a successful skill ultimately involves a personal expression.

The selection of a teacher also involves your developing a different kind of working relationship than you experienced during earlier periods. The mentors and rugged self-assertion of earlier stages of the life cycle no longer fit. You now need a companion to guide you. This person acts as a friend who shares certain skills with you.

None of the approaches to education in this stage of the life cycle needs to be costly. Most large communities have persons with the talents you seek and who may be willing to share their talents with you at little or no cost. A good way to find these people is to locate organizations of your interest. Libraries and community centers have a listing of various clubs and service organizations which can be useful in locating an organization that fits your needs. There are national organizations for virtually every interest imaginable, and these organizations almost always publish a magazine, booklet, or newsletter that is a source of general information as well as local clubs you might not be aware of.

I once attended an egg-decorating exhibition, showing the work of hundreds of persons. Before I attended the meeting I had no idea at all that anybody did these things, much less that there were formal organizations and regular regional and national meetings. I have also attended meetings for those interested in bird watching, model railroad, amateur soccer, bicycles, Thunderbird automobiles and many other activities.

Seminars provide another method of providing continuing education. Seminars often include a hundred or more people and no longer include only a few people in a workshop environment. A number of community colleges have begun to offer seminars on a wide variety of current topics. Some nationally recognized seminars are quite expensive, while locally sponsored private seminars usually carry only a nominal fee, and some are free. Seminars provide an excellent way of quickly expanding your knowledge of a subject and meeting other people with a similar interest.

You should carefully consider any hobbies that you have continued from an earlier stage of your life cycle. Often these hobbies reflect a dormant interest that takes hold in this period. In virtually every case that I have observed, the interests that are explored in this period have their roots in hobbies, pursuits, readings, or sports of earlier periods. Look in your attic, basement, or garage to see what you have kept from the past. It will often be a clue to your source of inspiration in this stage of the life cycle.

Entertainment

This, too, is a period of stress, and you need the friendship and the closeness of loved ones. At no other stage of the life cycle is loneliness so frightening and in many cases, so destructive. You should spend money for activities that provide you with the basis of making and maintaining friendships.

Entertainment expenses in this period of the life cycle mainly reflect spending with other people. This expense can be as minimal as buying cheese, crackers, and coffee to serve friends, a small gift for someone's birthday. It can be as costly as a world cruise on the Queen Elizabeth II. The settings are different, but the benefits from friendship are similar. The range of opportunities that are open to you are as large as your interests, and these interests are the source of direction to your entertainment activities.

Some people find the idea of spending money for entertainment difficult to follow. These people usually have been thrifty throughout their lives and look on entertainment as a somewhat frivolous activity.

These feelings sometimes reflect loneliness. Loneliness can be more paralyzing to your spirit now than during earlier stages of your life cycle, when you also had an introspective approach. Your physical energy is more limited during this period, and you cannot count on the momentum of that energy to carry you forward. At this time you need to use your knowledge of who you are to surmount loneliness. You need to use this knowledge to direct yourself in ways that will keep you out of the doldrums, and entertainment is a formal way of accomplishing that purpose.

Hospitality involves some expenditures, even if they are small. You should not allow your low level of finances, or your worry over the future, to be a reason to cut off all hospitality. Hospitality is an affirmation of your faith in your friends and the future. It expresses your faith that your friendship will endure. That is a powerful antidote to the loneliness that may accompany a turn to your inner thoughts. Your hospitality enables you to release your inner discoveries of this stage, so that they free you rather than hold you.

The key which never seems to fail to solve the apparent paradox of loneliness and a need to reach out lies in making little gifts to lots of people. Little gifts may seem like an unusual form of entertainment, but in its broadest sense, giving may be regarded as the supreme form of entertainment. The gifts provide a focus for interaction between you and others. Little gifts tend to convey all of the significance of large gifts, but they have the advantage of not placing the recipient in an embarassing position. Little gifts don't overwhelm, they give joy in quantities small enough to be completely acceptable.

One friend understood how to entertain magnificently with gifts. He knew his friends' interests well, and he noted everything he read or heard that pertained to these interests. Often this included a newspaper or a magazine clipping. Sometimes it included an out-of-print book or photograph, but the item never involved much expense. Whenever he read a paper, magazine, or passed a curio shop, he gave a scan for his friends. I would often, quite unexpectedly, receive a brief note in the mail together with an interesting clipping. His thoughtfulness was irresistable, and he held a large number of admirers in his sway. I asked once if he received as much satisfaction as I did when I received one of his notes and clippings. He answered, "Much more, because you can use this, while I can't." I will never be able to top that line.

Avocation

Making money is not an objective of this stage of the life cycle. But work is an essential part of life at all stages of the life cycle. You need work, because work provides you with a way of communicating with people around you in objective manner. Your family and friends give warmth and meaning to your life, while work gives it an identity and respect.

Instead of working for money in this period of your life cycle you should now work for enjoyment. You may not need to work for financial benefits in this stage if you have a combined income from Social Security and pension, savings, and investments that will keep bread on your table and a roof over your head. But the financial motive is only part of the motive for work. A far more energizing motive is our desire to see, in some material form, a reflection of ourselves. Our work is one way that we discover who we are.

This personal motive for work is no different during this age period of your life cycle than during other stages. But the motive is clearer for you to see, because many aspects of your life have become simpler. With the financial motive for work reduced, or no longer important, you can ask yourself what you really like to do. You should find the answer to be readily apparent.

Many people carry forward interests and hobbies that they had been thinking about for many years. This is the stage when you can try pursuits that you have long held in the background, because you felt that the interests did not fit into the image of your business. So far as work is concerned, this period of the life cycle is one of greatest freedom.

Work during this stage does not necessarily mean a typical eight-hour day. Most likely it means a part-time activity that involves a regular effort. Making money from your work is not essential. The motive that pushes you forward is enjoyment.

One friend retired from a relatively low-level position with a utility. He was a personable individual, and was always able to work with numbers easily. Nevertheless, he liked being busy more than he liked managing people, and so he never rose to a management level.

After he retired, he took a course in tax preparation which was given by a national tax service, and during the next tax season, he began to prepare individual tax returns. At first he felt limited by the amount of income he could earn without losing his Social Security benefits, but he found that he enjoyed the work so much that he reduced those benefits so that he could continue preparing taxes. After the tax season ended, he didn't stop studying taxes. He told me that he wished that he had taken this step years earlier. Perhaps he should have done so, because he has accumulated a considerable number of faithful clients in a very short time.

Another friend had spent a lifetime nurturing prize roses. She had developed a wealth of information about the way roses best grow, and she began to write a short bimonthly newsletter for her friends in various rose clubs. After a while, she offered to send the newsletter to rose growers throughout the country, and within a few years she built up the subscription of her newsletter so that it provided a modest but important income for her. This person is a slow, painstaking worker who would not fit easily into a commercial office. But that limitation doesn't affect her. She prepares the newsletter in her home and works at her own pace.

Investment Income

You should review your assets with an eye to transferring your nonincome-producing assets to income-producing assets. The changes you may make to increase your investment income during this stage of your life cycle may not be a burden, as they might have appeared during earlier stages. You now understand the meaning of traveling light and living light. You are freed from what you now see is a major burden of maintaining a large presence in your basic essentials.

You continue to need the essentials of life, such as food, shelter, and clothing. But in this period you do not need the quantity that you needed earlier. By scaling down amounts, you may be able to increase your investment income. A common example is when a person sells a large home and buys a smaller home in a less-expensive community. The transfer accomplishes two benefits. It reduces the operating costs of shelter, since a small home in a lower-tax-rate community probably will cost one-half or two-thirds less to operate than typical, larger homes in metropolitan areas. Moreover, the transfer frees assets from being nonincome producing to income producing. You can invest the difference between the sale of the old home and the purchase of the new home. Often this sum is quite substantial and can provide a major new source of income. Moreover, persons who are 55 years of age or older, and have lived in their home for three of the past five years, can exclude $100,000 of the profits of the sale of their home when they file taxes. Nevertheless, some persons have felt that the loss of old friends and social ties were not worth the financial benefits.

Most people are not able to save much during this stage of their life cycle, but a surprising number of people continue to do so. One person who lived quite humbly told me that she felt proud and more independent when she put a small amount in her savings account. She felt that her savings additions gave her a sense of control and assurance that she would be able to continue to be financially independent. Although the interest on her savings did not increase her income by much, she pointed out with pride that the interest covered her Christmas gifts.

The advantage of income from investments is that it gives you more flexibility in your budget. But you may still enjoy opportunities for personal enrichment, as long as your living costs are kept low.

Sometimes frugality actually increases clarity and brings unexpected benefits of greater personal insight. One friend in her seventies lives only from her social security in a senior citizens home. As a younger woman, she had traveled extensively in Asia. A mutual friend remarked that it was a shame that she had so little money to live with, and if she had more ample funds she would be able to travel. I wondered about that question, and I asked this woman if she ever wished to travel as she had previously. She replied that at one time she had thought so, but no longer. Her interest in travel was fully satisfied by her talks to service groups and schools. She felt that if she had funds to travel, she might not have developed her talks and her position in the community.

KEY ASSETS AND LIABILITIES

Money-Market Securities

Liquidity is an important objective of the management of your assets during this stage of your life-cycle. Liquidity gives you the opportunity to have funds available to use whenever needs arise.

The money-market assets providing the greatest liquidity are short-term money-market instruments, such as Treasury bills, certificates of deposit of major banks, or mutual funds that invest in these types of securities. These money-market investments can be sold immediately at a security broker's office or at the investment security department of a large bank. The mutual funds of money-market instruments usually provide check-writing privileges and can be quickly converted to cash.

If you make direct purchases of certificates of deposit in a large amount, you should choose banks with relatively high liquidity. If you purchase a certificate of deposit for an amount above $100,000, you should be sure that the bank has the liquidity in its assets to meet any major unexpected circumstance. Certificates of deposit larger than that amount are not covered by Federal Deposit Insurance Corporation guarantees. It is not necessary that a bank have the highest liquidity of all banks, but you should consider any bank carefully that does not rank in the upper half among comparable banks in liquidity. You should consider a bank which ranks in the lower third with considerable care. Banks with high liquidity usually offer certificates of deposit at approximately the same interest rates as those with low liquidity, so you do not have to pay a premium for this advantage. You may wish to ask a security analyst to provide you with liquidity comparisons of the banks in which you have an interest. Most security analysts can refer to standard tables and obtain the information in minutes.

In looking at several money-market mutual funds, read the prospectus of each carefully, as was noted earlier. These mutual funds buy a diverse variety of certificates of deposit, commercial paper and Treasury bills. Compare the objectives of the funds, and find the mutual fund that shares your objectives. The main objective in investing in bank certificates of deposit or commercial paper is safety of principal, since there are usually relatively small interest benefits from greater risk in these securities.

You should check the average maturities of the money-market mutual funds. You will want funds with relatively short average maturities, because short maturities protect the assets of the fund from sudden changes in value that could come from quick fluctuations in interest rates. Some funds have lengthened the maturity of their portfolio in order to show higher yield. Nevertheless, the higher yield of a fraction of a percentage point should not be regarded as compensation for this risk. You can make these maturity comparisons directly from prospectuses by yourself.

You should not purchase a money-market fund or any other mutual fund, that has a load fee built into its purchase price. A load fee is a sales commission that is subtracted from the money buying your assets. Sales charges represent money that is never going to work for you again. Studies have shown that the performance of stock mutual funds with load fees typically do not perform better than funds that do not have this sales charge.

Precious Metals

Some persons in this stage of the life cycle believe that escalating rates of inflation are inevitable and have responded by buying precious metals. These persons have experienced the devastating effects of inflation in their fixed income pensions, and they have seen sharp increases in the price of gold, silver, and platinum during the past decade. They also observe that precious metals provide liquidity that is as good as securities. They have turned to precious metals as a haven of security against inflation.

Holding precious metals does not provide current income, and metals involve some costs for storage. All financial gains come from capital gains. Since precious metals have risen sharply in price over the past decade, these gains have been strong.

If anything should change the inflation outlook, holders of precious metals should be prepared to sell their holdings. Yet the strong emotional convictions about holding these metals might keep them from doing so. If you hold precious metals, be sure that you try to keep an objective eye to what is happening to trends in inflation. The history of all markets, including those dependent on the outlook for inflation, is that directions which seem permanent eventually change. You would want to be sure that you pick up the signals of change early.

Stocks

Your interest in stocks may be a continuation from the maturity stage of the life cycle. During that earlier stage, you may have kindled an interest in stocks. In that earlier period, you looked at stocks from a broad perspective, particularly the prospects for capital appreciation. During the age and simplicity stage of your life cycle, you should look for stocks that are financially strong and pay generous returns. These stocks are not likely to provide unusual or sudden capital gains, but they should provide reliable income.

You should look for stocks of companies that have two key characteristics, a high dividend yield and a low debt-to-equity ratio. These stocks include firms that are some of the best entrenched, best managed, least risky companies among all companies.

A high dividend yield is important, because you now need current income. Your lower tax rate may tend to minimize the tax penalty of taking current dividends, rather than letting the company reinvest earnings and hopefully increase the value of your stock. Moreover, you may not be sure that the management of the company has as many good investment opportunities as it has funds available for investment. The reinvestment performance of companies is not uniform, and many companies have made investments and acquisitions in recent years that have lowered their profitability. You should get paid for your investment on a current basis. You should look for stocks that provide you with a good dividend.

A low debt-to-equity ratio gives you an indicator of whether the company is conservatively managed from a financial point of view. Conservatively financed companies seldom run out of money in a credit crunch, and typically have a low break-even point. When business conditions turn down, these companies meet reduced levels of business activity and still turn a profit. These conservative companies seldom make news headlines, seldom show sudden jumps in earnings, but they tend to be steady earners.

Making good stock decisions is a task at which people tend to get better as they get older. Younger people cannot bring your wealth of experience to bear on stock selection. You should use these capabilities to their fullest.

Real Estate

As was discussed earlier in this chapter, you may wish to sell your home if it is larger than your needs require and turn part of the value of this asset into other assets that generate current income. If you own an apartment or other income-producing property, you may wish to continue holding them, because they provide you with current income. Moreover, you may not wish to settle the tax liabilities that would be due.

However, if you own unimproved property, lots, or acreage that does not produce current income, you should consider selling them, and converting the money into income-producing assets. Many people in this stage of the life cycle find this difficult to consider. One member of my family had accumulated a wide variety of land holdings. He had been an attorney during the 1920s and when the depression of the 1930s arrived, many of his clients were unable to pay for his services in cash, so they deeded him land instead. One client of his had been an interurban street car company. He received a parcel from a bankruptcy court which measured 22 feet by one-half mile, and this land was virtually unuseable and unsalable. Yet this relative would not part with any of his property holdings. I believe that he had a certain personal attachment to the land, which gave him satisfaction each time he stood before it. I remember traveling with him to look at an 80-acre parcel. He stood before a field which led to a woods, and then to a river. It was almost as if he were imagining great deeds being accomplished on this land, perhaps a summer camp being built, a resort hotel, or a development of homes. I never knew, but I did know that he was crimped for money for living expenses, and the land returned nothing financial to him. The sale of this one parcel of land and reinvestment of the funds into income-producing assets would have been a significant help to his daily expenses.

There should be no rush to sell unimproved real estate during this stage of the life cycle. You should wait until the time is right. During the credit cycle, which typically lasts three to five years, credit markets alternate between periods of tightness, when interest rates are relatively high and money is difficult to borrow, and periods of ease, when interest rates are relatively low and money is easier to borrow. You should time the sale of the land for a period of credit ease. That would be a time when lenders would be most willing to make large loans at the best terms. The financing of real estate is often dependent on leverage terms, and you will find that during this period of the credit cycle, better leverage terms will be available than during any other period.

Antique Investments

A number of people in the age and simplicity period of their life cycle develop an interest to build a collection of antiques and fine objects of art. These people regard collecting as an activity that combines their personal interests and the financial benefits of asset appreciation. Many of these people also believe that antique collecting gives them an opportunity to leave their heirs something that is tasteful and more memorable than dollars.

You should group your antiques into two categories. The first group includes antiques that you use in everyday life and whatever items that you plan to leave to your heirs. These will comprise your personal collection. The second group includes items that you buy and sell on a trading basis. As you collect better or more interesting objects, you may wish to transfer certain less attractive items from your personal collection to your trading collection. But you will always keep a clear distinction between these two categories.

There will be no problems in handling your personal collection. The objects that you use in daily activities, such as furniture, carvings, or paintings, are needed in the way that you live. These are your treasures.

The objects you collect primarily for investment represent a different matter. These objects may be in your home, in a garage, or in a safe-deposit vault. You don't need them in your living, and you can easily replace them with something else, or even do without them. Your interest in those objects is primarily commercial.

You should consider trading these items, because these assets, like any other assets, will change in price. Antiques and collectibles are seldom priced in a uniform manner, and there are many undervalued and overvalued items. The under-valued items represent opportunities for trading profits, if you know the requirements of your markets well, have potential customers, and are current concerning trends and preferences.

This knowledge is not difficult to develop. Most people who collect antiques have acquaintances with a wide variety of dealers, restorers, wholesalers, and decorators. These people provide you with the information you need to make the right investment or trading decisions. Moreover, there are numerous magazines and newsletters that report on current trends and customer preferences. If you look to these sources, you should find the information you need to make profitable investments in antiques and collectibles.

Gifts and Wills

The final consideration of your assets is their disposition. The legal and accounting professions have provided a variety of ways of handling the disposition of assets to others. As was noted, these methods of handling assets have become more complex in recent years.

Despite this technical complexity, there is a basic issue concerning your assets that is important to persons in this period of their life cycle. The issue is whether to give away your assets during your lifetime or to give them away, as you must, when you die.

The traditional way of disposing of assets is through a will, which transfers funds at death. This method of trans-ferring your assets gives you the maximum present financial protection. You retain the current use of the assets, and you designate who will receive the assets after your death. Trusts provide ways of transferring funds during your lifetime, but they can be complex, and the emphasis in this stage of the life cycle should be simplicity. You should review both of these ways of transferring your assets. If you have accumulated sizeable assets which amount to a total that is clearly in excess of what you could need for the remainder of yours and your spouse's lives, wills and trusts may not be the best solution to the distribution of your assets. You may wish to make gifts while you are alive.

I have observed that people who make the best decisions concerning gifts are most reponsive and sensitive to the needs of others. This stage of the life cycle emphasizes simplicity and a live-and-let-live attitude. Any program that tends to be complex, or has the effect of tying other people to your commitment often fails. In making gifts, a freer, more open transfer of funds, without strings, works better.

You should use your powers of perception and intuition to see where a gift would provide the most benefit. People who are in touch with their children, relatives, and others and see what these people are trying to accomplish with their lives appear to be better able to know the impact that a gift of money could have on the lives of these people. When handled with sensitivity, gifts are beneficial to the recipient and the giver.

A key issue in making gifts is whether the gift would provide for consumption or for the development of the recipient. If the gift would provide for more expensive consumption, the benefits are likely to be transient. Gifts used to raise the standard of living of a recipient to a level that cannot be sustained tend to have a long-term negative effect. Gifts that provide for the self-development of the recipient usually have a beneficial effect. Gifts may be used for savings, investments, or business activities. In each instance the gift can provide a way of accelerating the personal development of the recipient. The gift is incorporated into that person's life, and thus it has personal significance.

The person who makes a gift should have an understanding of the effect a gift would have on the recipient before the gift is made. Moreover, the person who is prepared to make a gift may wish to help the potential recipient explore its use. This requires intuition and skill. Nevertheless, after the gift has been made, there must be complete freedom on the part of the recipient to use the gift without a sense of obligation, or the best benefits of the gift will be lost.

There is, of course, great pleasure to a giver in seeing a gift used in a way that provides focus to the self-development of a recipient. The financial benefits are only the means to that end. This pleasure can be the capstone to a life's activities. Money and assets, like any treasure, need to be used to enrich life and should be passed along when they can be more useful elsewhere. That approach is the philosophy of simplicity of this stage of the life cycle in its finest achievement.

PART *IV*
STARTING MONEY MANAGEMENT

Chapter 15

MONEY MUST BECOME YOUR SERVANT

*O*NCE you have made the decision to use money to unlock your personal resources, an important change in the role of money takes place. You see money as something that should work for you. The center of the stage is you, not money. This is the most crucial decision in money management you will ever make.

The key to making money work for you is to make your personal goals act as your control. Many people let their money do their buying. They are literally servants to money. They have not mastered control of themselves from a financial point of view, because they have not understood what is most important to them in life.

The control of your money is one of the most fundamental themes of personal money management. It has nothing to do with how many dollars you may have in the bank or what your net worth totals. It is an attitude toward yourself and

251

your money. It is, ultimately, a state of mind. It is the ability to direct your wants to personal development.

Still, control of your money must be measured in dollars. It must be demonstrated financially, to be sure that it does exist. It is simply spending less than you receive as income and building a savings pattern in your daily life.

The world is full of rich people who are broke, people who earn large sums of money and spend even more. One of the most surprising experiences of my life was when I reviewed the personal financial statements of applicants who wanted to open charge accounts in a summer job between years at college. This work involved gathering information about the income of people who had applied for credit with department stores and oil companies. I was a junior person and was only allowed to check department store credit. I was struck by the diversity in the way people handled their money and most of all, that spending habits often did not show a relationship with the ability to earn income. I had expected that people who wanted credit or needed credit would have small incomes. There were instances of this kind, but they were relatively few. There were many people who had large incomes, had already taken on large amounts of credit and debt, and wanted further credit. A few cases involved persons with incomes that, from my student's point of view, were a princely sum. These persons had accumulated debt service charges that would crimp their ability to service any new debt they might take on.

There is no end to the wants of most people. Some people want a better car, a longer vacation, more leisure, better sports, youthful looks, more freedom, not to mention more money. Yet more money, no matter how large the amount, will not solve the basic issues of personal money management.

You must face the issue of how to control your money. If you don't, others will control it for you. The matter is simple. Look at the people who run up bills. They perpetually face the credit controls placed on them by others. If they are delinquent in their payments, they will find that their credit lines will be frozen. If they apply for new credit, they may be turned down. If they ask for an advance from their employer, they may receive the advance, but the price they pay will be enormously high. Most employers make a mental negative note of any person who asks for an advance and mark the person as being unreliable with money. I have heard employers talk about persons who make requests for an advance and then shake their heads. Moreover, I have never known anybody who asked for an advance who subsequently received a promotion.

No matter what stage you may be in your life cycle, it is never too late to begin the practice of good money management. Opportunties may have been lost, but that doesn't matter. What matters for money management is the present and what you are building for the future. The power of your goals can change you and give you the strength to fulfill them.

Your achievement in managing money is its own reward. But there really is no other alternative. Your financial future lies not with your government, not with employer, and not with your customers. They will change and pass from view at some future time. Your financial future lies with yourself, and to fully achieve your personal destiny, money must become your servant.

(Continued from page iv)

Mr. James R. Robinson, Senior Vice President, Bank of America
Banker

Paul J. Brouwer, Ph.D., Director and Emeritus Partner,
Rohrer, Hibler & Replogle
Psychologist

Mr. Morgan W. White, President, The Portola Group, Inc.
Investment advisor

Mr. Dale Denson, President, Dalton Realty, Inc.
Realtor

Morton Glanz, M.D.
Physician

Mr. Kevin Boden, Host, KQED MoneyLine Show
Investment commentator